A NEW GUIDE TO THE BIRDS OF HONG KONG

A NEW GUIDE TO THE BIRDS OF HONG KONG

Michael Webster

Illustrated by Karen Phillipps

With an additional plate by Axel Olsson

SINO-AMERICAN PUBLISHING CO.
HONG KONG

First published in 1976 by
SINO-AMERICAN PUBLISHING CO.
114 How Ming Street
Kwun Tong, Kowloon,
Hong Kong

Second Edition 1977

ISBN 0 904917 01 0

© Michael Webster & Karen Phillipps 1976

Printed in Hong Kong by
CARITAS PRINTING TRAINING CENTRE

Colour plates and cover printed by
SHECK WAH TONG OFFSET PRINTING PRESS

INTRODUCTION

This book has been compiled solely to facilitate field identification of the birds of Hong Kong. All other aims have been subordinated to this, even to the extent that full descriptions have not always been given, in cases where there is no possibility of confusion with another species. The illustrations form an integral part of the descriptions, and should be used as such.

There is comparatively little published material on behaviour and call-notes of birds of this region, but as much detail as possible of these aspects has been included, where it is likely to help field identification. Brief descriptions of nest-sites and breeding dates have also been given.

Scientific names almost always follow King and Dickinson's "Field Guide to the Birds of South-East Asia", which in turn is based on Vaurie's "Birds of the Palaearctic Fauna". The order of families and species generally follows the "Annotated Checklist of the Birds of Hong Kong" (1975).

Vernacular names follow the Checklist (1975), again almost without exception. Names in brackets are those used in King and Dickinson, where they differ from the traditional Hong Kong names. If King and Dickinson's names become standard throughout South-East Asia, the older Hong Kong names will gradually go out of use. Some names have already been replaced in the Checklist (e.g. Black Bulbul for the old and misleading White-headed Black Bulbul).

This book does not attempt to replace the Checklist (1975), which should be consulted for an accurate statement of the status of rarities. While generally following the Checklist (1975), this book takes a more flexible viewpoint, giving full listing to a number of doubtful species, and hypothesising status where there is insufficient information for a definitive statement. This is done as a help for field use; for example, if a species is known to winter in Kwangtung, and yet has only been recorded a couple of times in Hong Kong, it might be described as 'Probable winter visitor', mentioning also the number of records. This is to save the necessity for reference to scarce books such as La Touche, to which most observers would not have access.

This book also describes, in brackets, species which may well occur in Hong Kong in the future. Claims to have seen such species should be treated with great caution.

Chinese names for each species have been taken from the 1975 edition of the Checklist, with additional names from Cheng Tso-hsin's numerous publications on Chinese birds. This work has been done almost entirely by Lawrence Tam.

When dates are given, these are dates when the species has occurred (for rarities), or dates when it normally occurs (for commoner species). These dates are for guidance only. It is unusual, but not extraordinary, to see species outside the normal dates of occurrence.

As species have been numbered to correspond with the plates, so that the latter can be used in both English and Chinese editions, it has not been possible to change the numbering to include new species. Such species have therefore been given 'a' numbers, but inserted in their proper place in the text.

The plates show almost every species genuinely found in the wild in Hong Kong, but it has not always been possible to show all states of plumage. It has also not been feasible to include all details of immature and intermediate plumages in the text; many of these can only be learnt by experience, though of course full descriptions should be taken of any birds which puzzle you.

G.A.C. Herklots' book "Hong Kong Birds", and the "Annotated Checklist" have been used as the basis for this field guide, and my debt to these is immense. The most important of the other books consulted are listed in the Bibliography. Individual members of the Hong Kong Bird Watching Society have given much help in various ways, in particular Ben F. King, F. O. P. Hechtel, John Gerson, and Richard Hale.

No field guide is ever complete; there are almost bound to be mistakes, which will become obvious as our knowledge of the birds increases. All comments are welcome, and an attempt will be made to improve the coverage in the next edition.

Equipment. You will need a good pair of binoculars, preferably between sizes 7 x 35 and 10 x 50. The quality must be good, as you will be using them for long periods in a day, and you can easily strain your eyes and get a headache if you use a pair with some defect. If you are not sure how to choose a good pair, buy a well-known brand; it may be more expensive, but at least you will be able to return it to the maker if something is wrong with it. As a general rule, the diameter of the object lens (the second figure given) should be at least five times the magnification (the first figure), or your binoculars will not be of much use in poor light. Larger sizes than 10 x are available, but it is difficult to hold these steady in the field.

A telescope is an optional extra, but is useful on the marshes and when looking out to sea. 30 x magnification is usually adequate; try to get one with a good tripod, so that you do not have to lie down to use it. Quite apart from getting dirty, you then find you cannot see over low vegetation.

You must take a notebook to record what you see and in particular to write down full details of any bird unfamiliar to you.

Make a habit of carrying your lunch with you, or at least plenty to drink, if you are out for a full day; this is particularly important in hot weather.

Wear dull-coloured clothes (to blend with the landscape as well as possible), and rubber-soled shoes (to reduce noise). Some kind of hat is advisable, especially if you are susceptible to sunburn. In summer you will need suntan lotion on the marshes, and antimosquito lotion in the woods.

Field observation. When you see an unfamiliar bird, you should try to note down the following:—

1. Size (by comparison with a common species), and general shape.
2. General colouration.
3. Conspicuous markings, e.g. eyestripe, coronal stripe, wingbar, any patch of a different colour.
4. Size and shape of bill.
5. Habits, where it perches, if it hops or runs, if it skulks, etc.
6. Flight... the way it flies, and any wingbars or other marks (e.g. forked tail, rump colour) noticeable in flight.
7. Habitat.
8. Song or call-notes.
9. Light conditions, and distance at which observed.

Make such notes regularly, and you will soon get into the habit of doing it, and, better still, you will notice these things sub-consciously on any bird you see. Make all your notes before you start looking at any books, then use this and other books to finalise your identification. It is fatally easy to imagine diagnostic features which were not there until you read about them in the book afterwards.

Societies. It is much easier, if less immediately satisfying, to learn your first birds from somebody more experienced. Generally, in Hong Kong, the only way to do this is to join the Hong Kong Bird Watching Society, c/o Zoology Dept., University of

Hong Kong, Hong Kong, which organises a dozen or more field trips every year. Members are always willing to help beginners, but you must be willing to learn; after all, it is hardly fair to expect an experienced birdwatcher to give you a lot of his time unless you make an effort yourself. Birdwatching in Hong Kong can be great fun, as we have great variety here, but much of it is hard work, and you have to be prepared for rough walking, and for days when nothing seems to go right.

Localities. The following are probably the best-known localities for birdwatching in the Colony, though there may well be others which have gone unnoticed.

1. Deep Bay Marshes, particularly the area between Chuk Yuen and Mai Po, and on to Lok Ma Chau.

    Part of this area, known as the Mai Po Marshes, has been a Restricted Area since June 1975, and you will need a permit to enter it. This is obtainable from the Agriculture and Fisheries Dept., Canton Road Government Offices, 393 Canton Road, Kowloon.

2. Mong Tseng Peninsula/Ping Shan, a large area of scrubland and marsh, with small hills overlooking Deep Bay.

3. Long Valley, by Lo Wu Camp, for eagles in winter.

4. The egretry at Yim Tso Ha, Sha Tau Kok, at the head of Starling Inlet.

5. The Lam Tsuen Valley, particularly the woods at She Shan, Tai Om, and Ma Po Mei.

6. The woods behind Sekkong Village.

7. The top of Tai Mo Shan.

8. Tai Po Kau Forestry Reserve.

9. The north side of Victoria Peak.

10. The woods round Jubilee Reservoir.

11. Ho Chung Valley in the Saikung Peninsula.

12. The wood beside the Stanley Military Cemetery.

ERRATA

Plate A. The bird numbered 12 is in fact species no. 22.
Plate E. Nos. 173 and 174 should be transposed.

Plate 1

Plate 2

New Guide to Hong Kong Birds

DIVERS: Gaviidae

Large swimming birds of the open sea. Long bodies, thick necks. Look hunchbacked in flight.

1. RED-THROATED DIVER *Gavia stellata*   Plate 1.

紅 喉 潛 鳥

21-24″. The only diver likely to occur here. Most noticeable character is apparently upturned bill. Flight rapid and direct. Slight white wingbar.

Three Hong Kong records, winter.

GREBES: Podicipedidae

Seabirds with dumpy bodies and longish necks (except Little Grebe). Swim and dive readily, but do not often fly. Head held low in flight.

2. GREAT CRESTED GREBE *Podiceps cristatus*   Plate 1.

鳳 頭 鸊 鷉

19″. Almost exclusively a seabird in Hong Kong. Distinctive silhouette with gleaming white cheeks and neck. Two conspicuous white patches show on wings in flight. In summer plumage, has dark frills either side of neck, and more prominent crest.

Regular in winter, particularly in Deep Bay, December to March.

3. RED-NECKED GREBE *Podiceps grisegena*   Plate 1.

赤 頸 鸊 鷉

17″. Almost exclusively a seabird in winter. Long dark neck, and shorter body distinguish from Great Crested Grebe at all seasons. Conspicuous white patch shows on wings in flight.

One record, January 1955.

4. LITTLE GREBE *Podiceps ruficollis*   Plate 1.

水 葫 蘆

10½″. Normally seen on fresh water. Dumpy body, short neck, brown, with whitish cheeks and deep maroon neck in summer. Call a prolonged trill. Nest built of floating vegetation in marshy areas; May and June.

Resident, mainly to be seen at Tai Lam Chung, Jubilee Reservoir, Plover Cove, and on the Deep Bay Marshes.

SHEARWATERS AND PETRELS: Procellariidae

Oceanic birds, generally seen flying close to the water, banking and turning on stiff pointed wings.

5. BULWER'S PETREL *Bulweria bulwerii*   Plate 1.
燕 鸌

11″. Brown, with a wedge-shaped tail. Very faint wingbar. Shape of tail distinguishes this from all other small Pacific shearwaters and petrels.

One sight record, May 1964.

6. SOOTY SHEARWATER *Puffinus griseus*   Plate 1.
灰 鸌

16″. Dark brown, with paler underside of wings. The latter is conspicuous as the bird tilts from side to side in flight.

One sight record, May 1973.

7. SWINHOE'S FORK-TAILED PETREL
(SWINHOE'S STORM-PETREL)   Plate 1.
Oceanodroma monorhis
黑叉尾海燕

10″. Entirely brown, with a deeply forked tail. Other possible vagrants include several similar species, but all have more extensive pale wingbars than Swinhoe's. Sight records unacceptable.

One specimen record, June 1961.

Unidentified albatrosses have been seen on occasions; possible species are Audubon's Albatross, *Diomedea nigripes*, which is entirely brown, paler below, and Steller's Albatross, *Diomedea albatrus*, which has underparts white, and some white on wings.

PELICANS: Pelecanidae

Huge birds, marine in winter, with long bills and conspicuous gular pouches. Generally in flocks. According to some authorities, the two Hong Kong species are conspecific.

8. SPOTTED-BILLED PELICAN (SPOT-BILLED PELICAN)
Pelecanus philippensis   Plate 2.
斑 嘴 鵜 鶘

Up to 60″. Off-white plumage with pinkish gular pouch, this being darker in summer. Safest distinction is flight-pattern; primaries and a wedge across the rear edge of the underwing are black, the rest white. Immatures are browner, but still show darker primaries.

Winter visitor to Deep Bay, December to March.

9. DALMATIAN PELICAN *Pelecanus crispus*   **Plate 2.**
捲 羽 鵜 鶘

Up to 72″. Whiter than the Spotted-billed Pelican; gular pouch orange in breeding plumage, yellow in winter. In flight, primaries and tips of secondaries are blackish when seen from above; only tips of primaries are black on underwing, which is otherwise completely white.

Winter visitor to Deep Bay, December to March.

CORMORANTS: Phalacrocoracidae

Black sea-birds, with long hook-tipped bills. Dive frequently.

10. (GREAT) CORMORANT *Phalacrocorax carbo*   **Plate 2.**
鸕　鷀

36″. Black, with white patch on thighs. In breeding plumage, almost complete head and neck are white. Underparts white on immatures. Often seen perched on rocks, with wings hanging out to dry. Large flocks fly in line ahead formation.

Winter visitor to Deep Bay, other marine areas, and Tai Lam Chung; November to March.

(RESPLENDENT SHAG (PELAGIC CORMORANT) *Phalacrocorax pelagicus,* 30″; black, with white patch on thighs, and, in breeding season only, white streaks on head and neck. At other seasons, only safe distinction is the reddish warts on the bare facial skin; distinguished from *P. urile* only by less massive bill. Hong Kong records before 1939, unsubstantiated).

FRIGATE-BIRDS: Fregatidae

Piratical oceanic birds; dark with long narrow wings and deeply forked tails. Most unlikely to be seen except in flight (soar for hours on end).

11. GREAT FRIGATE-BIRD *Fregata minor*   **Plate 2.**
軍　艦　鳥

34-40″. Large size and shape distinguish frigate-birds from all other birds. Male of this species is entirely black except for a dark band on the wings; female has white breast and throat. Vagrant in Hong Kong waters, May to September.

12. CHRISTMAS ISLAND FRIGATE-BIRD   **Plate 2**
(CHRISTMAS FRIGATE-BIRD)
Fregata andrewsi

聖誕島軍艦鳥

35-40″. Distinguished from the last by dark throat and white abdomen in all adult plumages.

One record, May 1971.

(**LESSER FRIGATE-BIRD** *Fregata ariel*, 32″; the male has a conspicuous white patch on either side of the body under the wing; otherwise entirely dark; female has dark throat, white breast and front part only of abdomen; could occur).
(These notes on frigate-birds apply to adults only; immatures are not easily separable).

HERONS, EGRETS, and BITTERNS: Ardeidae

Long-legged marsh birds, large. Often skulking or crepuscular. Most Herons and Egrets nest in large colonies; nests built of sticks up to 100 ft. up in trees. Colonies often mixed. Bitterns not always colonial nesters, nest on ground in thick reed-beds. Neck tucked back on shoulders in flight. Deep wingbeat, especially Herons and Bitterns.

13. VON SCHRENCK'S LITTLE BITTERN (SCHRENCK'S BITTERN) **Plate A.**
Ixobrychus eurhythmus
紫背葦鳽
12-13″. Chestnut above; wings dark grey tinged chestnut; chin white; rest of underparts buff. Male has buffish, female has whitish spots on back and shoulders. Male has dark line down centre of pale throat, and dark patch at base of neck. Crepuscular.
Four records, all 1956 and 1957, April, September, and October.

14. YELLOW BITTERN *Ixobrychus sinensis* **Plate A.**
小水駱駝
13-14″. Yellowish-brown, with darker wing-tips. Underparts paler, though depth of colour of upperparts varies considerably. Frequently seen perched on tops of reeds. Nest built of reeds near the ground in a reed-bed; April to August.
Common summer visitor to marshy areas of Hong Kong, with quite a few winter records. Mainly April to October.

15. CHESTNUT BITTERN (CINNAMON BITTERN)
Ixobrychus cinnamomeus **Plate A.**
栗葦鳽
15-16″. Male brilliant chestnut, paler below. Female chestnut-brown, streaked paler, with black streaks on underparts. Breeding as for Yellow Bittern.
Summer visitor to marshy areas in small numbers, April to September.

16. BLACK BITTERN *Dupetor flavicollis*   **Plate A.**
黑　鳽
22″. Male black, with orange patch on side of neck, whitish
chin and front of neck. Female duller, brownish-grey. Largely
crepuscular. Almost annual in summer on the Deep Bay
Marshes, where it may breed, April to September.

17. JAPANESE NIGHT HERON *Gorsachius goisagi* **Plate A.**
栗頭虎班鳽
23″. Head and back chestnut, darker on crown; wings dark
brown. Underparts buff, with a dark streak from base of bill
down centre of abdomen; heavy streaking on abdomen and
flanks. Crepuscular; restricted to damp woodland localities,
where it seeks food on the ground.
Two records, December 1972 and November 1974.

18. (GREAT) BITTERN *Botaurus stellaris*   **Plate A.**
水　駱　駝
30″. Brown, richly mottled and streaked blackish. Crepuscular.
Rarely seen unless flushed, when it flies slowly just above reed-
level. Distinguish from immature Night-Heron by dark streaking
(instead of whitish spots) on upperparts, and larger size.
Winter visitor to the Deep Bay Marshes, November to March.

19. (BLACK-CROWNED) NIGHT HERON   **Plate A.**
　　　　Nycticorax nycticorax
夜　　鷺
24″. Black crown and back; white forehead and underparts;
grey wings and tail; chiefly crepuscular. Young birds are brown,
can be confused with Bittern in flight, but always distinguished
by pale tips to feathers of wings, forming three broken wingbars.
Passage migrant; a few breed (since 1972). March to October.

20. CHINESE POND-HERON *Ardeola bacchus*   **Plate 3.**
池　　鷺
21-24″. Chestnut-red head, breast and back, white wings and
underparts. The white is not visible when the bird is at rest.
In winter, the chestnut-red is replaced with buff, streaked brown.
Builds nest of sticks, generally in the lower levels of the egretry.
Resident, with an increase in numbers in summer.

21. CATTLE EGRET *Bubulcus ibis*   **Plate 3.**
牛　背　鷺
20-23″. Orange head and neck distinguish from all other egrets
in breeding plumage. All white for the rest of the year. Bill

and facial skin always yellow, legs and feet black. Nest as Chinese Pond-Heron, but usually higher in the trees. Often feeds among grazing cattle.

Summer visitor, with winter records. March to November.

22. LITTLE GREEN HERON (LITTLE HERON)   Plate A.
Butorides striatus
綠　　鷺

14-15″. Crown black (slight crest), upperparts slaty-green, underparts whitish, streaked with grey. Black moustache stripe. Looks uniformly dark in flight, but is much smaller than Black Bittern. Legs dull yellow to orange. Often prefers coastal mangroves. Autumn visitor, but has bred, and is occasionally seen in winter. May to October.

23. LITTLE EGRET *Egretta garzetta*   Plate 3.
白　　鷺

22″. All white. Narrow crest-plumes; thick plumes on back. Noticeably shorter than Lesser Egret. Bill black; facial skin greyish; legs black; feet bright yellow. Very slender bill. Yellow feet easily seen in flight. Nest as Chinese Pond-Heron, but generally higher up the tree.

Common resident in the north of the New Territories.

24. LESSER EGRET (PLUMED EGRET)   Plate 3.
Egretta intermedia
中　白　鷺

20-23″. All white. Plumes on crest and back. Bill yellow, sometimes with black tip, and noticeably stubby; facial skin yellow; legs and feet black.

Occasional visitor. May, September to December.

25. SWINHOE'S EGRET (CHINESE EGRET)   Plate 3.
Egretta eulophotes
黃 嘴 白 鷺

21″. All white. Plumes on crest, back, and breast. Bill orange-yellow and quite thick; facial skin blue; upper two-thirds of leg black, remainder yellow. Leg colour varies between this and completely greenish-brown in mid-winter. Nest as Little Egret. Summer visitor; a few pairs annually. April to August.

26. (PACIFIC) REEF EGRET *Egretta sacra*   Plate 4.
岩　　鷺

20″. Slate-grey, with a white streak down the throat. Lemon-yellow legs. A bird of rocky coasts, not normally seen in marshy land. Builds a nest of sticks among rocks not far above the tideline. Resident round the coast.

(**Note:**— a white form of this species also exists, but reports of this form probably result from confusion with other egrets on migration, when the Cattle Egret in particular has been seen on rocky coasts.)

27. GREAT EGRET *Egretta alba*   **Plate 4.**

大 白 鷺

33-36″. All white. Plumes on back only. Bill yellow in winter, yellow tipped with black in spring, and greenish-black in summer; facial skin greenish-yellow; legs and feet black. Much larger than all other egrets.

Winter visitor; has bred; frequent summer records.

28. GREY HERON *Ardea cinerea*   **Plate 4.**

蒼 鷺

36″. Very large; basically pale grey; neck almost white. In flight, pale grey body and most of wings contrast strongly with black primaries. Often in flocks.

Winter visitor with occasional summer records. October to March.

29. PURPLE HERON *Ardea purpurea*   **Plate 4.**

紫 鷺

31″. Can only be confused with Grey Heron, from which it is distinguished by its predominantly reddish-brown colouration, very thin neck, and, in flight, comparative lack of contrast between primaries and the rest of the upperparts. Usually solitary or in pairs.

Passage migrant, with frequent summer and winter records. September to May.

STORKS: Ciconiidae

Large black and white heron-like birds. Neck outstretched and slightly drooped in flight. Flock formation irregular (Cranes fly in V-formation).

30. ORIENTAL WHITE STORK *Ciconia boyciana*   **Plate 4.**

白 鸛

About 45″. Primaries, secondaries, and scapulars black; rest white. Bill black, legs and feet red. (Black bill distinguishes from White Stork *Ciconia ciconia*, which could occur, but has bright red bill.)

Two records in winter, February and March.

31. BLACK STORK *Ciconia nigra*　　　　　　　**Plate 4.**
烏　　鸛
38″. Glossy black upperparts, throat, and breast; underparts
below breast white. Bill, legs, and feet scarlet. In flight, white
belly on otherwise all-black bird, and cruciform shape (the
longest part being the neck) are distinctive even at a great
distance. Often in small parties.
Winter visitor to the Deep Bay Marshes. November to March.

SPOONBILLS AND IBISES: Threskiornithidae

Large wading birds, with curved or flattened bills. Necks outstretched in flight.

32. GLOSSY IBIS *Plegadis falcinellus*　　　　**Plate 3.**
彩　　環
22″. Almost black, glossed with purple, bronze, and green. Bill
long and decurved. Note rounded wings in flight.
One sight record, September 1953.

33. WHITE IBIS (BLACK-HEADED IBIS)　　　　**Plate 3.**
　　　Threskiornis melanocephalus
白　　䴉
24″. Long decurved bill, head and neck black and unfeathered.
Remainder creamy-white, with a little black on scapulars and
tips of primaries. Immatures are greyer.
Winter visitor to the Deep Bay Marshes, September to April.

34. (WHITE) SPOONBILL *Platalea leucorodia*　　**Plate 3.**
琵　　鷺
33″. White. As Lesser Spoonbill, but the spoon of the bill is
yellow, and the facial skin is yellow with a black line across it.
Probably rare passage migrant and winter visitor (first identified
in 1975).

35. LESSER SPOONBILL　　　　　　　　　　　**Plate 3.**
　　　(BLACK-FACED SPOONBILL)
　　　Platalea minor
黑 臉 琵 鷺
30″. White. All black or dark grey spoon-shaped bill is
diagnostic. Black triangle of facial skin is visible from a distance. In summer, has bushy white crest and orange gorget.
Immatures have black tips to wings. Feeds by sweeping bill
from side to side.
Passage migrant and winter visitor; October to March.

Plate 3

Plate 4

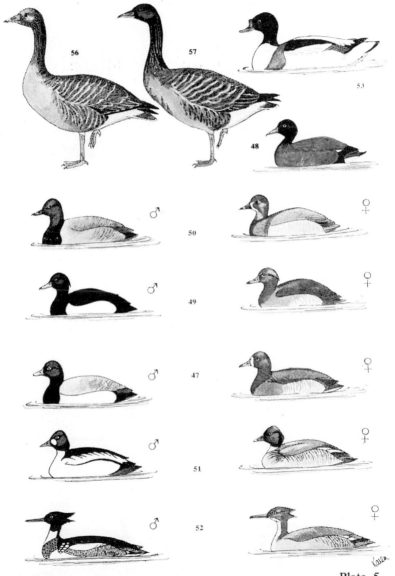

56 57 53 48

50 ♂

♀ 50

49 ♂

♀ 49

47 ♂

♀ 47

51 ♂

♀ 51

52 ♂

♀ 52

Karen

Plate 5

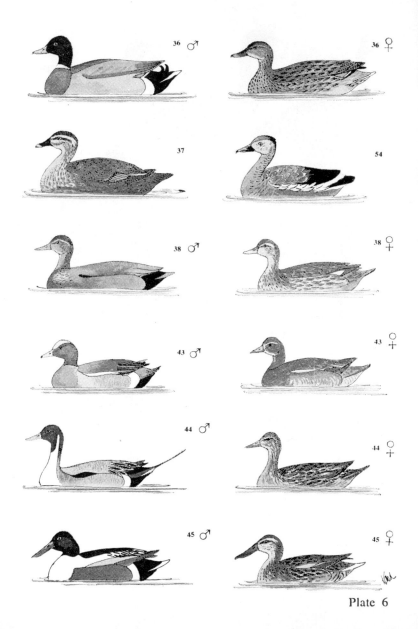

36 ♂   36 ♀
37   54
38 ♂   38 ♀
43 ♂   43 ♀
44 ♂   44 ♀
45 ♂   45 ♀

Plate 6

DUCK: some genera of the Anatidae

Medium to large waterfowl, very variable in habits. Brightly-coloured speculum is important characteristic in flight. Many species go into eclipse plumage after breeding; that is, males look very like females in autumn.

36. MALLARD *Anas platyrhynchos*   **Plates 6, 8.**

綠 頭 鴨

23″. Male has green head, white collar, brown breast, black and white tail, largely greyish-buff body. Female and male in eclipse brown. Violet-blue speculum seen in flight, between two white wing-bars. See Yellownib Duck.
Scarce winter visitor. October to March.

37. YELLOWNIB DUCK (SPOTBILLED DUCK)
　　Anas poecilorhyncha   **Plates 6, 8.**

斑 嘴 鴨

23″. At close range, whitish eyebrow and black yellow-tipped bill distinguish from female Mallard, from which it is otherwise almost indistinguishable. Purple speculum. White patch on wing formed by tips of tertiaries. (In Japanese birds, of the same subspecies, dark belly is diagnostic in flight; this does not seem to apply in Hong Kong.)
The commonest large duck in winter on the Deep Bay Marshes. August to April.

38. GADWALL *Anas strepera*   **Plates 6, 8.**

紫 膀 鴨

20″. Grey male, with black under tail providing contrast even at some distance; female similar to female Pintail, but has shorter tail. Red-brown, black, and white speculum; white is conspicuous in flight on both sexes.
Scarce winter visitor to the Deep Bay Marshes, September to March.

39. FALCATED TEAL *Anas falcata*   **Plate 7.**

羅 紋 鴨

18″. Male has chestnut and green head and crest, white chin, narrow black collar bordered below with white; body primarily mottled grey, with drooping scapulars. Female mottled brown. Speculum dark green, black in female; white bar in front of speculum, and white collar, are marks to look for in flight. Head looks huge when crest is erected.
Regular in winter in Deep Bay, probably more maritime than other teal. October to March.

40. (COMMON) TEAL *Anas crecca*   Plates 7, 8.
綠 翼 鴨

14″. Small. Male has chestnut head with green eyepatch, grey body with white stripe above wing, and a conspicuous yellow spot below black tail. Female and eclipse male are brown with green speculum. In flight, looks very dark, with two narrow white wingbars. Flocks fly fast, keep in compact formation. Takes off almost vertically.

Common winter visitor. September to March.

41. BAIKAL TEAL *Anas formosa*   Plate 7.
花 臉 鴨

16½″. Male unmistakable; largely brown, with darker head; buff cheeks vertically bisected by black line. Female brown, with white spot at base of bill, pale cheeks and whitish chin; dark line through eye, a broken pale line above the eye. Green speculum. In flight, very dark, with narrow white line behind speculum.

Two records, both shot. February, October.

42. GARGANEY *Anas querquedula*   Plates 7, 8.
白 眉 鴨

15″. Small. White eyestripe, very pronounced in male, less so in female, is easiest distinction from Teal. Speculum indistinct. In flight, blue-grey shoulders of male are conspicuous, and double wingbar is more pronounced than in Teal. Habits similar to Teal.

Passage migrant on the Deep Bay Marshes. August to October and March to May.

43. (EURASIAN) WIGEON *Anas penelope*   Plates 6, 8.
赤 鸝 鴨

18″. Chestnut head, buff crown, grey body distinguish male. Female only safely distinguishable at close range by bluish bill, and by smaller size than Mallard, Gadwall, and Yellownib. Speculum dark green, almost black in female. In flight, distinguished by white shoulders and belly in male, pale shoulders in female.

Winter visitor. October to March.

44. (COMMON) PINTAIL *Anas acuta*   Plates 6, 8.
針 尾 鴨

22″. Male has chocolate head, with long white streak down either side, to white throat and breast, grey body and long pointed tail. Female very similar to Wigeon, Gadwall, etc., as

pointed tail is sometimes insufficient to distinguish. In flight, noticeably slender; light border to rear of speculum is best feature when no breeding-plumaged males are present.
Winter visitor. October to February.

45. (NORTHERN) SHOVELER *Anas clypeata*   **Plates 6, 8.**
琶 嘴 鴨
20″. Spoon-like bill is good mark under all conditions. Male has green head, white breast, chestnut sides; female is brown. Bluish shoulder-patches are noticeable on both sexes in flight. Sits very low in water, with bill pointing downwards.
Scarce winter visitor to the Deep Bay Marshes. October to March.

46. MANDARIN DUCK *Aix galericulata*   **Plate 7.**
鴛 鴦
17″. Orange whiskers, orange sails most outstanding characteristics of very colourful male. Female is grey, with white spots on breast, white marks behind eye and around bill. Generally in pairs. Perches on trees, rocks. Generally found by the edges of rocky streams, not on open water.
Three records (two shot). November.

47. (GREATER) SCAUP *Aythya marila*   **Plates 5, 8.**
斑 背 鴨
19″. Male is black at both ends, pale grey in the middle. Female like female Tufted, but has large white patch at base of bill. Grey, not black, back distinguishes from Tufted in flight. Broad white wingbar in flight. Largely maritime in habit.
About six records. December, January.

48. BAER'S POCHARD *Aythya baeri*   **Plate 5.**
青 頭 鴨
16″. Dark mahogany brown, with paler belly. Green gloss on head of fully adult male. Conspicuous white patch below tail. Curved white wingbar in flight. Male has white eyes. Female is similar but duller. Wedge-like shaped head helps to distinguish this species from rather similar Tufted Duck.
One shot out of three seen, February 1972; seen, January 1976.

49. TUFTED DUCK *Aythya fuligula*   **Plates 5, 8.**
鳳 頭 鴨
17″. Male black with white sides; female dark brown, with small white patch at base of bill. Broad white wingbar in flight. Normally on fresh water. Dives frequently.
Scarce winter visitor to the Deep Bay Marshes and Plover Cove. November to February.

50. COMMON POCHARD *Aythya ferina*   **Plates 5, 8.**

紅 頭 鴨

18″. Male has chestnut head, black breast, grey body. Female has brown head and breast, pale brown body, without streaking or mottling. Broad grey wingbar in flight. Grey speculum. One sight record, a male, May to June 1970.

(RED-CRESTED POCHARD *Netta rufina* could occur; 22″, paler head, red (instead of bluish-grey) bill, and white sides distinguish male from Common Pochard; female has pale cheeks and a red spot on the bill; note black underparts of male in flight.)

51. (COMMON) GOLDENEYE   **Plates 5, 8.**
    Bucephala clangula

金 眼 鴨

18″. Male black above, white below, with white spot behind bill. White scapulars, streaked black. Female has dark brown head, white collar, grey body. Note shape of head. In flight, inner half of wing, and, in male, two lines down body, white, with little black marking.

Three records (one shot). November, December.

52. RED-BREASTED MERGANSER   **Plates 5, 8.**
    Mergus serrator

紅胸秋沙鴨

23″. Exclusively maritime in winter. Long low-slung body can only be confused with divers or cormorants. Male has dark green head and crest, white neck, chestnut collar, black back, grey and white sides. Female is grey-brown, with chestnut crown and hindneck grading into white throat. In flight, inner half of wing almost entirely white in male, with two narrow black lines across it; in female, speculum and feathers behind it are white. Long thin neck and bill are easiest flight distinctions from other duck.

Winter visitor to Deep Bay, occasionally on other coasts; December to March.

(CHINESE MERGANSER (SCALY-SIDED MERGANSER)
Mergus squamatus, 24″, differs from above in having pronounced scaly markings on flanks, though these are often obscured in autumn; very long narrow crest; no chestnut patch at base of neck; underparts entirely white; prefers fresh water; could occur.)

53. (COMMON) SHELDUCK *Tadorna tadorna*   Plates 5, 8.
冠　鴨

24″. Greenish-black head, white body with broad chestnut band round forepart. Scapulars and primaries black; speculum green, legs pink, bill red (with prominent knob in males). In flight, it is the only duck with almost completely white tail, and a white wedge up the back.

Winter visitor to the mouth of the Shum Chun River. December to March.

54. LESSER WHISTLING TEAL   Plate 6.
(LESSER TREEDUCK) *Dendrocygna javanica*
樹　鴨

16″. Chestnut-brown, darker on wings with pale chestnut underparts. Very slight wingbar. In flight, appears dark above and below, with no conspicuous markings. Buff superciliary can be helpful at close range. Looks more like a small goose both on ground and in flight. Neck slightly hunched in flight. Rounded wings.

About five records (one trapped). April to October.

55. COTTON TEAL (COTTON PYGMY GOOSE)   Plate 7.
Nettapus coromandelianus
棉　鳧

13″. Very small. Male has head, neck and underparts white, brown crown, black collar round base of neck, back and wings dark green. Female browner, with a brown eyestripe, no collar, and greenish tinge to brown wings. In flight, male shows a white patch on the wing.

One shot, September 1969; one seen, October 1974.

GEESE: some genera of the Anatidae

Large noisy waterfowl; feed largely on land. Migrate in V-formation.

56. GREY-LAG GOOSE *Anser anser*   Plate 5.
灰　雁

30-35″. Brown, with white barring on wings. All grey geese look much alike in the field, and the points to look for on Grey-Lags are pink bill and legs, no white forehead, no black on bill, head and neck rather pale, front part of wing very pale in flight.

Four records, possibly annual in winter. November, March.

(**(GREATER) WHITE-FRONTED GOOSE** *Anser albifrons* may occur; 26-30″, white forehead, pinkish bill, orange legs, heavy dark barring on belly, are the points to look for.)

57. BEAN GOOSE *Anser fabalis*   **Plate 5.**

大 雁

28-35″. Distinguish from Grey-Lag by two-tone black and yellow bill, orange legs and feet. Generally the darkest of the grey geese; head and neck look black at a distance. Wings uniformly dark in flight.

One shot, February 1955; one seen, December 1974.

HAWKS, EAGLES, HARRIERS: Accipitridae

Includes all diurnal birds of prey but Osprey and Falcons; generally large, soaring frequently. For identification, flight patterns are essential in most cases.

58. BLACK-EARED KITE (BLACK KITE)   **Plates B, 9.**
      Milvus migrans

麻 鷹

23″. Slightly forked tail is best distinction. Generally dark brown, with pale patch at base of primaries; habit of using tail as rudder is helpful (Buzzard also does this sometimes). Commonly seen soaring in thermals or drifting along mountain ranges; scavenges in Hong Kong Harbour. Builds large stick nest, usually in a tree; January to April. Call, a trembling scream.

Resident; numbers augmented in winter, when communal roosts become very large.

(**BRAHMINY KITE** *Haliastur indus*, 18″, has been recorded twice. The second bird was certainly an escape, as probably was the first, as the species is normally sedentary. Can only be confused in shape with Black Kite, but white head and breast, and bright chestnut wings, body, and tail are unmistakable; habits similar.)

59. BLACK BAZA *Aviceda leuphotes*   **Plate 9.**

鳳 頭 鵑 鷹

12-13″. Upperparts and upper breast black; conspicuous crest. White wing-patches. Underparts below breast white, with chestnut band across lower breast, and some chestnut barring below it. White wing-patch in flight is diagnostic. Flight weak. Silhouette like a falcon. A forest hawk. •

One record, May 1972.

(**CRESTED HONEY BUZZARD** *Pernis ptilorhynchus*, 25-27″, similar to other Buzzards, but distinguishable by broad dark subterminal band on tail, and two narrower dark bands near under tail-coverts; a forest bird; one obtained in Macau.)

60. (COMMON) BUZZARD *Buteo buteo*   Plates B, 9.
鵟

22-24″. Plumage highly variable. Flight silhouette of broad wings and ample rounded tail is best guide (round tail distinguishes from Black-eared Kite, wings held level from Marsh Harrier, both of which are similar in size). The commonest and most distinctive plumage phase in Hong Kong shows dark patches below carpal joints, and dark band across belly, underparts being otherwise pale; tail faintly barred. Hovers occasionally.

Common winter visitor; September to March.

(**ROUGH-LEGGED BUZZARD** *Buteo lagopus*, 20-25″, has been recorded four times, but these were probably Buzzards of the plumage-phase described above; this is similar to typical Rough-legged, but Rough-legged has the belly-band higher up, and almost always has near-white tail with more or less pronounced dark terminal band; hovers frequently; Rough-legged does not normally wander so far south. **UPLAND BUZZARD** *Buteo hemilasius*, 28″, is larger and paler than either; pale russet underwing with whitish patch near carpal joint, barred tail; hovers frequently. **LONG-LEGGED BUZZARD** *Buteo rufinus*, 24-26″, has completely unbarred tail, and cinnamon-coloured underparts. The plumages of all four Buzzards are not well known as far as the Eastern races are concerned, but known distribution makes occurrence of all but the Buzzard unlikely.)

61. (NORTHERN) SPARROWHAWK   Plates C, 10.
Accipiter nisus
鷂

12-15″. Short rounded wings and long tail distinguish from all but the two following species. Size, and barring on underparts distinguish from Horsfield's Goshawk, and size and slight whitish superciliary are the principal distinctions from Japanese Sparrowhawk. Upperparts slate-grey on male, dark brown on female (much the larger); underparts barred, often rufous in adult male. Like most *Accipiter* spp., a woodland species.

Scarce passage migrant and winter visitor; October to March.

62. JAPANESE SPARROWHAWK — Plates C, 10.
Accipiter gularis

松 雀 鷹

10-12". Distinguished from Sparrowhawk mainly by size. Mesial streak conspicuous on juvenile. Adult male has pinkish underparts, barred pale grey; no superciliary. Underparts heavily barred on juvenile. In hand, fourth primary longest, third and fifth equal. Indistinguishable in the field from the **BESRA** *Accipiter virgatus*, 12-14", which has fourth and fifth primaries equal, third between these and sixth. Coastal mangroves on migration.

One specimen record in 1966, all other records being doubtful because of confusion with Besra (Besra is non-migratory, and morphological differences may be due to this rather than to it being a separate species).

63. (NORTHERN) GOSHAWK — Plates C, 10.
Accipiter gentilis

蒼 鷹

19-24". Female much the larger, almost Buzzard-size. At rest, dark eyestripe and prominent white superciliary are distinctive. In flight, short, rounded wings, almost white underneath, closely barred with slate; conspicuous white under tail-coverts; tail with three or four dark bars. Juvenile is paler, and streaked, not barred, below. Principally a woodland bird, but sometimes soars.

Passage migrant in small numbers, with possibly occasional birds wintering; March, November.

64. HORSFIELD'S GOSHAWK (CHINESE GOSHAWK)
Accipiter soloensis — Plates C, 10.

赤 腹 鷹

10-12". Like a miniature Goshawk, but wings comparatively pointed in flight, and with less conspicuous superciliary; in adults, underparts are neither barred nor streaked, being white tinged reddish. In flight, looks pure white below, with black wingtips. Young birds have chin and throat white streaked with grey, with prominent dark mesial streak; underparts more rufous than adults, with pronounced spots on the breast, bars on the flanks, or uniform.

Two or more records on spring passage; April.

65. GOLDEN EAGLE *Aquila chrysaetos* — Plate 11.

金 鵰

32-37". Immature has distinctive white tail with broad dark terminal band. Adults are very dark, with golden tinge on head and nape, only visible at close quarters. Sub-adults have

Plate 7

Plate 8

Plate 9

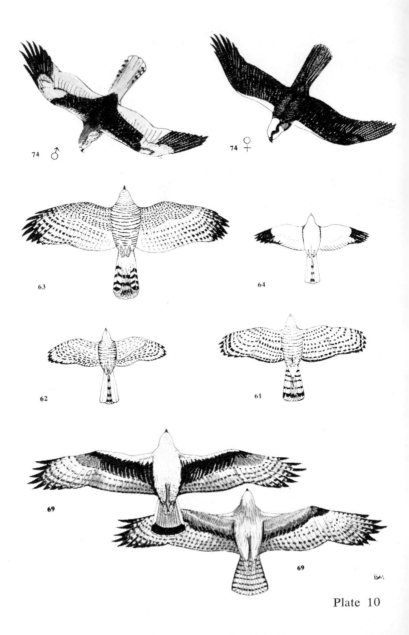

74 ♂

74 ♀

63

64

62

61

69

69

Plate 10

white patch at base of primaries. Extreme care should be taken with all identifications of eagles, as light conditions can confuse even the most apparently obvious characters.

Winter visitor in small numbers; November to March.

66. IMPERIAL EAGLE *Aquila heliaca*　　　　**Plate 11.**
白 肩 鵰

31-33″. Pale yellow crown and nape, and white scapulars (showing in flight as white lines on the upperwing either side of the body) distinguish fully adult birds. Very young birds are pale fawn, with streaked breasts and whitish upper tail-coverts. Longer wings than Spotted. Soars frequently. Birds between second and fifth years can be distinguished in the field from sub-adult Golden by lack of white patches at base of primaries, and closely-barred tail. Usually these also show some white on scapulars. Wings slightly angled upwards from body (head-on view).

Winter visitor in small numbers; November to March.

67. STEPPE EAGLE *Aquila rapax*　　　　**Plate 11.**
草 原 鵰

29-32″. Adults are almost uniformly dark, only safely distinguishable from Spotted by yellowish patch on nape. Immatures are paler, with dark primaries; head and throat pale and unstreaked. White on upper tail-coverts of some birds. Patchy appearance of wings in flight is diagnostic of immatures. Plumage very variable. Wings held horizontal in flight.

Winter visitor in small numbers; December to March.

68. (GREATER) SPOTTED EAGLE *Aquila clanga* **Plate 11.**
烏 鵰

26-29″. Compact dark eagles, showing a little white on upper tail-coverts of some, but not all, adults. First and second year birds show considerable white spotting on upperparts. Often soaring, but also spend much time perched on the ground. Wingtips point slightly downward in flight (head-on view).

Winter visitor in small numbers; November to March.

(MOUNTAIN HAWK-EAGLE *Spizaetus nipalensis* 30″, upperparts brown, with long crest; throat whitish, with pronounced mesial streak; underparts pale brown, barred with white; immatures whiter below; a bird of mountain forests; may occur.)

69. BONELLI'S EAGLE *Hieraeetus fasciatus*   **Plates C, 10.**

白 腹 山 鵰

26-29″. Dark brown upperparts and underwing contrasting with white underparts distinguish adult. In juvenile, underparts are rusty brown, giving a uniformly dark appearance. In flight it is like a long-winged Buzzard, the white underparts showing clearly on an adult, but no distinguishing marks on a juvenile. Broad black terminal band to tail of adult or sub-adult, faint in juvenile. Open country.

Probably resident in very small numbers.

70. WHITE-TAILED EAGLE *Haliaeetus albicilla*   **Plate 11.**

白 尾 海 鵰

30″. Pure white wedge-shaped tail on an otherwise brown eagle (head is pale brown and mottled) should be diagnostic for adults. Immature is all brown, including tail. Soars on straight wings like a vulture. Catches fish on surface.

Seven or eight records, open to some doubt because of possible confusion with immatures of the next species.

71. WHITE-BELLIED SEA-EAGLE   **Plate 11.**
Haliaeetus leucogaster

白 腹 海 鵰

30″. Adult has white head, underparts, and tip of tail, remainder slate-grey. Immature birds are largely brown, with paler head, and whitish tail tipped darker; underparts buffish to white. Tail is wedge-shaped. Wings usually sharply angled in flight. Huge nest of sticks built on a cliff, and added to year after year; December to February.

A few pairs resident.

72. GREY-FACED BUZZARD-EAGLE   **Plates B, 9.**
(GREY-FACED BUZZARD)
Butastur indicus

屎 鷹

17″. Greyish head, white throat, sometimes with mesial streak, brown breast, abdomen barred brown and white, vent white; upperparts rich dark brown. Easiest to recognise in flight by almost pointed wings and long tail, making it look like a gigantic broad-winged falcon.

Scarce passage migrant; March, April, October, November.

73. (CRESTED) SERPENT EAGLE   Plates C, 11.
Spilornis cheela

蛇 鵰

26″. Black crest, spotted white; upperparts dark brown, underparts russet, with whitish spots. In flight, very broad rounded
wings with three rows of whitish spots along hindwing; tail
black with one broad and one narrow grey band. Screaming
call, especially during courtship. Often perches high in a dead
tree. Flight pattern from underneath shows a broad white band
in wings and tail.

Scarce winter visitor in woodland areas; October to April.

74. MARSH HARRIER *Circus aeruginosus*   Plates C, 10.
澤 鵟

21-23″. Much heavier build than Hen Harrier, with pronounced
angle to wings in flight. Male is brown, with grey on wing and
tail, dark primaries, pale head; sometimes very similar to Pied,
but lacks black on breast. Young males are extremely variable,
often showing much cream or grey around head and shoulders,
and white rump. Females are brown above, with, sometimes,
cream head, and sometimes also white rump. Rectrices barred.
Much heavier build should provide immediate distinction from
Hen Harrier, and there is much more risk of confusion with a
Buzzard or Black-eared Kite (q.v.).

Common winter visitor to the Deep Bay Marshes; September to
April.

75. PIED HARRIER *Circus melanoleucos*   Plates B, 9.
鵲 鵟

18-20″. Male has head, upper breast, back, primaries, and
scapulars black, the rest pale grey above, white below. Shape
similar to Marsh Harrier (q.v.), generally flies higher above reedbeds, and often soars. Female distinguished from Marsh by
streaking on abdomen.

Scarce winter visitor; November to March.

76. HEN HARRIER (NORTHERN HARRIER)   Plates B, 9.
Circus cyaneus

白 尾 鵟

17-20″. Harriers are long-winged, long-tailed hawks usually seen
quartering a marsh or mountainside. Wings held at a pronounced angle, with primaries curving up slightly. Male Hen is grey,
with white rump, dark primaries. Female is brown, with white
rump, four black bars on chestnut tail. Very slender wings
distinguish this from both Pied and Marsh. Juvenile has streaked
underparts.

Scarce winter visitor to the Deep Bay Marshes; October to March.

(MONTAGU'S HARRIER *Circus pygargus;* one sight record of a female in 1908; as this species is virtually indistinguishable, in female or immature plumage, from Hen, and this is well outside the species' known range, this record must be considered doubtful.)

77. BLACK VULTURE (CINEREOUS VULTURE) Plate 11.
Aegypius monachus

禿　鷲

39-42″. Vast, very dark, with long, almost straight, wings, and wedgeshaped tail. Very large spread primaries. Brown ruff, head and neck bare. Usually seen soaring.

Scarce winter visitor; December to March.

OSPREY: Pandionidae

78. OSPREY *Pandion haliaetus* Plates B, 9.

魚　鷹

20-23″. Dark upperparts, white underparts; white head, with black patch through eye. Wings slightly bow-shaped in flight. Hovers over water, and plunges feet-first for fish. Spends much of day perched on stakes, etc., in the shallows. Often seen carrying a fish, held parallel to the bird's body.

Winter visitor to Deep Bay and Plover Cove; September to April. Occasional in summer.

FALCONS: Falconidae

Smallish, sharp-winged hawks, characterised by swift flight. Males generally slaty, females brown above.

79. WHITE-LEGGED FALCONET (PIED FALCONET)
Microhierax melanoleucos Plate 12.

小　隼

7″. Tiny; upperparts largely black; white superciliary, forehead, and underparts. Primaries and underside of tail conspicuously spotted white. Slightly larger than a Chinese Bulbul; will capture birds almost its own size on the wing.

One sight record, November 1952.

80. (NORTHERN) HOBBY *Falco subbuteo*　　　**Plate 12.**
燕　隼

12-14″. Like miniature Peregrine, with chestnut on thighs and beneath tail; tail closely barred, underparts heavily streaked. Long wings and short tail. A bird of woodlands.

Scarce passage migrant; March, October, November.

(ORIENTAL HOBBY *Falco severus*, 10″, is very similar to Hobby, but has much more black on head, no moustache stripe, and chestnut underparts from the breast down.)

81. PEREGRINE FALCON *Falco peregrinus*　　　**Plate 12.**
遊　隼

15-19″. Large size, rapid pigeon-like flight, and pronounced black moustache stripe distinguish from other falcons. Underparts barred (streaked in juvenile). Builds nest of sticks on a cliff in March, April; same eyrie used year after year.

Resident and winter visitor in small numbers.

(SAKER FALCON *Falco cherrug*, 18″, resembles dark female Peregrine, reddish-brown with whitish crown and nape; underparts lightly spotted; moustache stripe narrow and pale; the one sight record, in 1953, is doubtful, as no description survives, and the bird would be well outside known range.)

82. MERLIN *Falco columbarius*　　　**Plate 12.**
灰　背　隼

10½-13″. Like Hobby, but no moustache stripe. Underparts rufous, heavily streaked, but nothing like as bright as Hobby. Broad black subterminal band to tail. Proportionately much longer tail than Hobby, so is actually considerably smaller. A bird of open country. Generally flies low over ground or bushes.

Scarce passage migrant, possibly winter visitor; November to February.

83. AMUR FALCON *Falco amurensis*　　　**Plate 12.**
紅　脚　隼

12″. Formerly considered a race of Red-footed Falcon *Falco vespertinus*, which it closely resembles. Male is entirely slate-grey, with orange bill, eyepatch, thighs, feet, and white wing-lining. Female has barred grey back, russet crown, and rufous belly. Often hovers.

Two records; October, December.

84. (EURASIAN) KESTREL *Falco tinnunculus* Plate 12.
紅 隼

13½″. Head, rump, and tail grey on the male, with black subterminal bar to tail; rufous upperparts and long tail distinguish from other falcons; female larger and browner. Habitually hovers. Normally in open country, often on bare hillsides. Common winter visitor; September to March.

PARTRIDGES AND QUAIL: Phasianidae

Terrestrial birds, plump. Flight rapid, with very fast wingbeat.

85. CHINESE FRANCOLIN *Francolinus pintadeanus* Plate 13.
鷓 鴣

12-13″. The only partridge in Hong Kong; black eyestripe, white cheeks and chin patch, with a black line running diagonally from the bill; plumage otherwise basically brown, spotted with white. Rasping call heard freely in spring from bare rocky hillsides, where the cock perches on a rock and calls repeatedly. Otherwise rarely seen. Nests on the ground, often in a tussock or under a bush; April to June.

Resident, common on bare hillsides.

86. JAPANESE QUAIL *Coturnix japonica* Plate 13.
鵪 鶉

6½″. Small, plump, brown above, paler below; whitish superciliary and two black marks on side of neck distinguish from button-quails. Skulks in grassland. Often in small parties.
Passage migrant, possibly some wintering; October to April.

87. RING-NECKED PHEASANT
(COMMON PHEASANT) *Phasianus colchicus*
環頸雉(雉雞)

21-35″, including 8-20″ of tail. Long pointed tail; male chestnut with green head; female mottled brown.
Extinct locally.

BUTTON-QUAILS: Turnicidae

Small plump birds of paddy and grassy hills. Skulking, and rarely seen unless flushed. Females more brightly coloured than males.

88. BARRED BUTTON-QUAIL *Turnix suscitator*   **Plate 13.**
棕 三 趾 鶉
6-7″. Black breast in spring (female only), white for rest of year; barred, not spotted, underparts are best distinction from Yellow-legged Button-Quail. Legs are blue-grey.
Scarce winter visitor; October to March.

89. YELLOW-LEGGED BUTTON-QUAIL   **Plate 13.**
        Turnix tanki
黃脚三趾鶉
5-6″. Brown, streaked and spotted whitish; breast chestnut, spotted with black; legs yellow.
Scarce winter visitor; October to March.

CRANES: Gruidae

Large Heron-like birds, chiefly terrestrial. Neck extended in flight. Flocks fly in V-formation.

90. COMMON CRANE *Grus grus*   **Plate 4.**
灰鶴(蕃薯鶴)
45″. A huge grey bird, with darker feathers drooping over tail; head and upper neck black, with scarlet patch on crown, and white stripe running down the neck from the eye. Black primaries and secondaries seen in flight, when legs trail well beyond the tail. Cf. Grey Heron.
Six records; October to December.

RAILS: Rallidae

Skulking marsh birds, with short rounded wings, short tails. Legs dangle in normal flight, but Rails are capable of flying at considerable heights and for long distances. Young are generally black, downy, leave nest almost immediately after hatching.

91. WATER RAIL *Rallus aquaticus*   **Plate 13.**
秧　鷄
11″. Brown streaked black upperparts, with grey throat and whitish underparts; black and white barred flanks; long red bill. Crown is brownish-grey. Skulking, but sometimes comes out on open mud. Largely crepuscular.
Winter visitor to the Deep Bay Marshes; October to March.

92. BANDED RAIL (SLATY-BREASTED RAIL)   Plate 13.
Rallus striatus

灰 胸 秧 鷄

10″. Distinguished from similar Water Rail by chestnut crown, and less red on bill. Nests on ground in or near clumps of reeds; April to June.

Resident on the Deep Bay Marshes, probably in some numbers.

93. BAILLON'S CRAKE   *Porzana pusilla*   Plate 13.

小 田 鷄

7″. A small brown crake, streaked with white above; under-parts grey to white, with barring under vent; white patch on the throat. Distinguish from very similar **YELLOW-LEGGED CRAKE** *Porzana exquisita* by green instead of yellowish-flesh legs, and lack of chestnut band across breast.

About four records of birds captured or shot; April, September and October.

94. RUDDY CRAKE (RUDDY-BREASTED CRAKE)
Porzana fusca   Plate 13.

紅 胸 田 鷄

8″. Upperparts unmarked olive-brown; chin white, throat and breast vinous; rest of underparts barred brown and white. Legs red.

Probably regular in small numbers on passage; April, May, September, October.

95. CRIMSON-LEGGED CRAKE (BROWN CRAKE)
Amaurornis akool   Plate 13.

紅脚苦惡鳥

11-12″. Upperparts olive-brown; chin and throat white; sides of neck and rest of underparts blue-grey; legs and feet carmine. Prefers the small streams between paddy-fields. Nests in thick grass or reeds; April.

Irregular summer visitor; April to August.

96. WHITE-BREASTED WATERHEN   Plate 13.
Amaurornis phoenicurus

白 面 鷄

12-13″. Upperparts mainly slate-grey; forehead, sides of neck throat, breast, and abdomen white; flanks and vent bright chest-nut; legs greenish. Nests in bushes about 3 ft. off the ground, generally near a stream; April to May.

Common resident in low-lying areas.

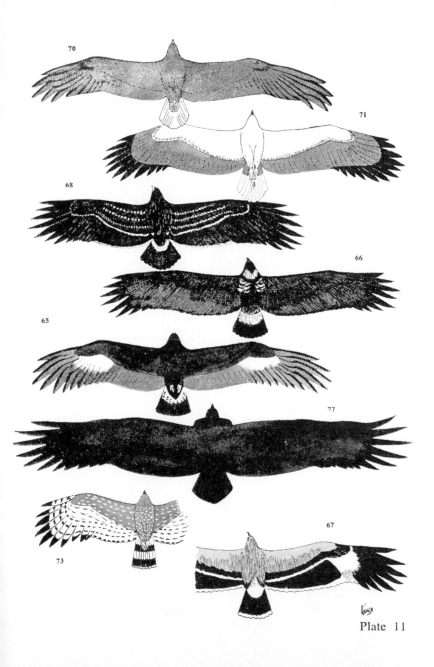

Plate 11

79

80

81

Juv.

ADULT

80

81

82

♂ ♀

82

♀

83

♂

83

♂ 84 ♀

84

Plate 12

Plate 13

Plate 14

97. (COMMON) MOORHEN *Gallinula chloropus*   **Plate 13.**

黑 水 雞

13″. Black, with red frontal shield and bill, white streak across flanks, and white under tail-coverts. Juvenile browner, with whitish underparts. Swims jerkily, jerking head and tail when alarmed. Builds nest of sticks and reeds close to the water, often in a reedbed; April to August.

Resident in the Deep Bay Marshes and Long Valley, the numbers being higher in summer.

98. WATERCOCK *Gallicrex cinerea*   **Plate 13.**

董 雞

13-16″. Male black, with red frontal shield and horn, and white leading edge to wing; female brown and striated. Distinguished from all other rails by the prominent horn of the male, upright stance, and flight silhouette; neck is long and outstretched, legs stretched out behind like a longish pointed tail. Breeding as Moorhen; May and June.

Summer visitor to the Deep Bay Marshes; April to November.

99. (COMMON) COOT *Fulica atra*   **Plate 13.**

白 骨 頂

15″. Black, with white frontal shield. Gregarious; easily disturbed, when it flies to a considerable height. Other rails fly low down except on migration. Flight silhouette as Watercock, but Watercock keep closely to the reedy areas, whereas Coot tend to swim in open water.

Winter visitor, sometimes in large numbers. Occasionally on the sea. October to March. Some summer records.

JACANAS: Jacanidae

Characterised by extremely long toes, which enable them to walk over floating vegetation. Otherwise rail-like.

100. PHEASANT-TAILED JACANA   **Plate 14.**
Hydrophasianus chirurgus

水 雉

12″ in winter, 18″ in summer (10″ being tail). Black and white, with golden patch on back of neck, and long droopy black tail. Brownish in winter plumage. In flight wings are largely white, with dark primaries; in summer, primaries are only tipped black. Floating nest attached to reeds, or on marshy ground; May to August.

Passage migrant, and summer visitor since 1968; April to November.

PAINTED SNIPE: Rostratulidae

Birds of marshy areas, generally preferring thicker cover than true snipe.

101. (GREATER) PAINTED SNIPE   Plate 14.
Rostratula benghalensis
彩　鷸

10-11″. Long red bill; yellow coronal stripe; white eyering with short white line behind it; upperparts are brown, heavily marked with buff; underparts white, streaked on breast. Female in summer plumage has deep chestnut breast, bordered with black below. In flight, no wingbar; note V-shaped white mark on back (male only), and slow buoyant wingbeat. Tail-patches in flight appear similar to those of Ruff.
Winter visitor in marshy areas; September to March.

OYSTERCATCHERS: Haematopodidae

102. (COMMON) OYSTERCATCHER   Plates 14, 19.
Haematopus ostralegus
蠣鷸（都鳥）

17″. Large; black and white plumage, orange-red bill, pink legs, make this unmistakeable. Prominent white wingbar and rump on otherwise black upperparts in flight.
One sight record, December 1958.

PLOVERS: Charadriidae subfamily Charadriinae

Stout, short-billed shorebirds, generally preferring sandy areas (Lapwings and Asiatic Golden Plover sometimes prefer grass).

103. (NORTHERN) LAPWING   Plates 14, 20.
Vanellus vanellus
鳳　頭　麥　鷄

12″. Black with green sheen; cheeks and belly white; prominent wispy crest. In flight, broad black rounded wings, white rump, and black subterminal band to tail.
Scarce winter visitor; December to February.

104. GREY-HEADED LAPWING   Plates 14, 20.
Vanellus cinereus
灰　頭　麥　鷄

14″. Grey-brown upperparts, grey breast, white abdomen. Bill yellow tipped black is conspicuous. Conspicuous yellow eyering. In flight, grey upperparts with black primaries and white secondaries are diagnostic; wings are pointed (by comparison with Lapwing).

Winter visitor, scarce; October to March.

105. HARTING'S RINGED PLOVER
(LONG-BILLED PLOVER)　　　　Plates D, 20.
Charadrius placidus

劍鴴，長咀鴴

8″. Complete black gorget (incomplete and brown on juvenile), no white above black forehead-band. Pale yellow legs. Longer black bill and larger size should distinguish immediately. One white wingbar. A bird of stony streams, not mudflats.

One record, December 1955.

106. LITTLE RINGED PLOVER　　　　Plates D, 20.
Charadrius dubius

黑　領　鴴

6″. Complete black gorget (incomplete and brown in juvenile), white line above black forehead-band. Yellowish legs. No wingbar in flight. Passage migrant and winter visitor, with occasional records in all months; October to April.

(COMMON RINGED PLOVER *Charadrius hiaticula* 7″, resembles Little Ringed Plover, but has wingbar, no white line above black forehead-band; no records.)

107. KENTISH PLOVER　　　　Plates D, 20.
Charadrius alexandrinus

千鳥（ 白鴴 ）

6″. Gorget on sides of breast only, very sharply defined in summer plumage. Rufous crown. Dark legs; one white wingbar; these two points distinguish birds of all ages from Little Ringed Plover. Shape is also more compact.

Passage migrant and winter visitor. August to May.

108. GREATER SAND-PLOVER　　　　Plates D, 20.
Charadrius leschenaultii

鐵 嘴 沙 鴴

8½ ″. See following species. Longer bill, and more upright appearance. Both species have a white wingbar.

Passage migrant, much commoner than Mongolian Sand-Plover; April to June, August to October.

109. MONGOLIAN SAND-PLOVER
(MONGOLIAN PLOVER)
Plates D, 20.

Charadrius mongolus

蒙 古 沙 鷸

7½". Very similar to Greater Sand-Plover. Distinguish by shorter bill, much more compact appearance. In summer, male usually has black line dividing white throat from chestnut breast, and more chestnut on the breast than the Greater Sand-Plover. In all other plumages, considerable experience is needed before you can tell the two species apart, unless both are present in the same flock, as bill-length is the only really safe guide.

Passage migrant in small numbers; April to June, August to October.

110. ORIENTAL PLOVER *Charadrius veredus*　Plates D, 20.

紅 胸 鷸

9-9½". A large plover; long legs; male in spring has white cheeks, deep chestnut breast separated by black line from white belly; upperparts brown with darker primaries. Female has buff cheeks and underparts, breastband slightly darker than rest of underparts. Faint white wingbar. Prefers grasslands, and not normally found on marshes. General shape like Golden Plover, not like sand-plovers.

Irregular passage migrant; March to May, September.

111. GREY PLOVER *Pluvialis squatarola*　Plates D, 20.

灰 斑 鷸

11". Similar to Asiatic Golden Plover, but larger and greyer; upperparts black and silver in summer. Best field mark is black axillaries (armpits) in flight. Call, three notes 'tlee-oo-ee'. Forms small flocks.

Winter visitor to the marshes; September to April.

112. ASIATIC GOLDEN PLOVER
(LESSER GOLDEN PLOVER)
Plates D, 20.

Pluvialis dominicus

金 錢 鷸

9". Upperparts golden spangled with black, underparts largely black in spring. In winter plumage, underparts are white, and upperparts are duller. One faint wingbar. Callnote a liquid 'tlui'. Usually in flocks.

Passage migrant on marshes and fields; March to May, September to November.

113. (RUDDY) TURNSTONE   Plates D, 20.
Arenaria interpres

翻 石 鷸

9″. Plump; white head with black markings, bright orange-chestnut and black back. In winter, head, breast, and upper-parts are dark grey, chin and abdomen white. Bright orange legs. For diagnostic wing-pattern, see Plate 20.
Passage migrant on the marshes; April, May, August, September.

SANDPIPERS, CURLEWS, GODWITS, SNIPE: Charadriidae subfamily Scolopacinae
Principally long-legged wading birds with long slender bills.

114. FANTAIL SNIPE (COMMON SNIPE)   Plates 16, 17.
Gallinago gallinago

扇 尾 鷸

10½″. Distinguished from other snipe by white trailing edge to wing in flight. In the hand, Fantail Snipe has seven pairs of rectrices, all fairly broad, with no appreciable white.
Mainly on passage, some winter; September to April.

115. PINTAIL SNIPE *Gallinago stenura*   Plates 16, 17.
針 尾 鷸

10½″. Not safely distinguishable from other snipe in the field. In the hand, has twelve pairs of rectrices, the seven outer pairs being very narrow, like pins, 2-3 mm. wide.
Winter visitor; September to April.

116. SWINHOE'S SNIPE *Gallinago megala*   Plates 16, 17.
大 沙 錐

11½″. Slower, heavier flight than Pintail, but doubtfully distinguishable in the field, though considerably larger in the hand. In the hand, has ten pairs of rectrices, the seven outer ones narrow, about 4-5 mm. compared with 2-3 mm. on Pintail.
Passage migrant and winter visitor; September to April.

(LATHAM'S SNIPE *Gallinago hardwickii* is similar to the three above, but prefers dryer country; tail has nine pairs of rectrices, graduated in size, the outer ones heavily barred; Swinhoe's is most similar, but has no barring on outer rectrices.)

117. SOLITARY SNIPE *Gallinago solitaria*   Plates 16, 17.
孤 沙 錐

12″. Much paler than other snipe, with practically no black on plumage. Keeps to overgrown streams, grassy hillsides, and upland paddies. Flies like Woodcock when flushed; heavy, rather slow, with wings somewhat rounded.

One formal record, and one sight record, but reports of several others shot; February.

118. JACK SNIPE *Lymnocryptes minimus*　　　Plates 16, 17.
小　鷸

7½". Small size and characteristic snipe shape distinguish from all others. Bill is also relatively much shorter. Usually silent when flushed.

Three records, but probably shot almost annually; March, April.

119. (EURASIAN) WOODCOCK　　　Plates 16, 17.
Scolopax rusticola

丘　鷸

13½". A woodland species, rarely seen unless flushed. Rounded wings and triangular head-shape distinguish from all snipe, which it resembles in plumage (brown streaked and spotted darker, with black bars on head and neck). Crepuscular.

Winter visitor; October to March.

120. (EURASIAN) CURLEW *Numenius arquata* Plates 16, 19.
白 腰 杓 鷸

21-23". Long decurved bill and striated brown plumage separate Curlews and Whimbrels from other waders. In flight, Curlew has white V up back. See other species for distinctions. Call a loud 'coorliu'. Curlew and Australian Curlew are larger than any other waders.

Winter visitor; September to April.

121. AUSTRALIAN CURLEW (EASTERN CURLEW)
Numenius madagascariensis　　　Plates 16, 19.

大　杓　鷸

23". Even longer bill than Curlew. No white on back or rump. Otherwise as Curlew. Call as Curlew, but harsher.

About eleven records, nine on spring migration; April, September.

122. WHIMBREL *Numenius phaeopus*　　　Plates 16, 19.
中　杓　鷸

16". Like a small Curlew, with shorter bill. Prominently striped crown. Call is a rippling series of six to eight notes. Back and rump white, sometimes almost obscured by brown streaking.

Passage migrant; April, May, September, October.

123. LITTLE WHIMBREL (LITTLE CURLEW)
Numenius minutus   **Plates 16, 19.**

小 杓 鷸

11½". Much smaller than Whimbrel. Bill shorter than Whimbrel, only slightly decurved. No white on back or rump.
Four records. May, October.

124. BLACK-TAILED GODWIT *Limosa limosa* **Plates 14, 19.**
黑 尾 鷸

16". Long straight bill (red at base, black at tip) and large size distinguish from all other waders (Bar-tailed Godwit has slightly upturned bill). In summer, neck and breast are pale chestnut, and flanks are barred blackish. In flight, prominent white wingbar and black subterminal band on white tail are conspicuous. Call 'wicka-wicka-wicka' not often heard.
Passage migrant; March, April, September, October.

125. BAR-TAILED GODWIT *Limosa lapponica* **Plates 14, 19.**
斑 尾 鷸

15". Distinguish from Black-tailed Godwit by slightly upturned bill, shorter legs. In summer, male is rich reddish chestnut, covering whole underside; female duller. In flight, Eastern form shows pale rump and wingbar, but no white on rump; this pattern is very similar to the Asian Dowitcher, but Bar-tailed Godwit has red bill tipped black, whereas Dowitcher's is all black. In winter both Godwits are pale grey, mottled, with whitish underparts, and difficult to tell apart except in flight.
Scarce passage migrant; March, April, September, October.

126. ASIAN DOWITCHER   **Plates 14, 19.**
Limnodromus semipalmatus

半 蹼 鷸

13". Rather Godwit-like, but with a very long heavy bill, slightly broadened at the tip. Brown above, with pale feather-edgings; in summer, red head and breast. Underparts white. Legs shorter than Godwit's. In flight, pale greyish rump and wingbar. Bill and legs black. Feeding by rapid stabbing in the mud is often a good field mark.
Irregular passage migrant; April, August, September.

127. GREEN SANDPIPER *Tringa ochropus* **Plates 15, 17.**
白腰泥岸鷸

9". In size, between Common Sandpiper and Redshank. In flight, sharp contrast between dark wings and body and white rump; underwings dark. No wingbar. On the ground, distin-

guished from Wood Sandpiper by darker, less speckled upperparts. Dark greenish legs. Call a liquid 'chuit, wit-wit'.
Winter visitor, preferring grassy areas and stream-banks; September to April.

128. WOOD SANDPIPER *Tringa glareola*   Plates 15, 17.
林 鷸

8″. Distinguish from Green Sandpiper by more speckled upperparts, and yellowish legs; in flight, underwings are pale. No
wingbar. Very noisy, making a distinctive trilling in flight;
gregarious (Green Sandpiper is normally solitary or in small
parties). Prefers open marsh.
Common passage migrant, some winter; August to May.

129. (COMMON) REDSHANK *Tringa totanus*   Plates 15, 17.
赤 足 鷸

11″. Generally browner than Spotted Redshank, but best distinction is prominent white rear edge to wing in flight. Red legs.
Wide variety of musical notes, including a rapid 'teu-teu-teu';
calls loud and excited. Summer plumage similar to winter, but
browner and more streaked, especially on breast and flanks.
Passage migrant, with a few winter records; April, May, August
to October.

130. SPOTTED REDSHANK *Tringa erythropus* Plates 15, 17.
赤 足 鶴 鷸

12″. In summer, black underparts, and upperparts black spotted with white, distinguish from all other waders of similar size.
Red legs. In winter, very similar to Redshank, from which it
can be distinguished by longer bill, longer legs, and lack of
wingbar. Trailing edge of wing shows paler, but not white, in
flight. 'Tchooit' flight call is helpful.
Winter visitor and passage migrant; October to May.

131. (COMMON) GREENSHANK   Plates 15, 17.
Tringa nebularia
青 脚 鷸

12″. Contrast between dark wings and white body distinguish
from Redshank which it resembles in shape. Legs green. For
distinctions from Marsh Sandpiper and Nordmann's Greenshank,
see under those species. Ringing call-note resembles that of
Redshank, but is usually on only one tone. In flight, white V
up back is similar to Spotted Redshank, but Greenshank can be
distinguished by contrast between dark wings and light body.
Passage migrant and winter visitor; August to May.

Kace Phillips

Plate 15

Plate 16

114—117

101

118

119

132

129

130

131

127

128

127

128

133

152

Plate 17

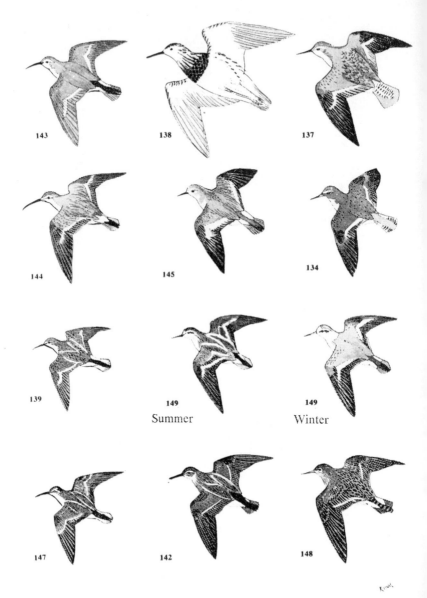

143

138

137

144

145

134

139

149
Summer

149
Winter

147

142

148

Plate 18

132. NORDMANN'S GREENSHANK Plates 15, 17.
Tringa guttifer

小 青 脚 鷸

11″. Very difficult to distinguish from Greenshank. Shorter legs, yellow base to lower mandible, and call-notes are best guide. Calls, a sharp scream, and a quiet 'cheep'. Less excitable than Greenshank, and does not usually fly high when disturbed.

Two records; September, May.

133. MARSH SANDPIPER *Tringa stagnatilis* Plates 15, 17.

澤 鷸

9″. Like a small slender Greenshank, with noticeably small head, and needle-like bill. Legs greenish. Looks very spotted in summer. Feverishly active. Feet project well beyond tail in flight. Call a series of twittering notes.

Passage migrant; April, May, September, October.

134. COMMON SANDPIPER Plates 15, 18.
Actitis hypoleucos

磯 鷸

8″. Plain brown upperparts, white underparts, with light brown patch at side of breast. White wingbar and sides of upper tail coverts. Characteristic fluttering flight low over water. Usually seen at the edges of streams or ponds, where it constantly bobs its head and tail. Call, a tuneless twitter. Not gregarious.

Passage migrant and winter visitor; August to May.

135. GREY-RUMPED SANDPIPER Plates 16, 20.
(GREY-TAILED TATTLER)
Heteroscelus brevipes

灰 鷸

10″. Plain grey above, without wingbar or rump-patch; underparts white, finely barred grey in summer. Slight eyestripe. Rather short bill. Legs yellow. Shows preference for dryer areas of sand.

Passage migrant; April, May, August to October.

136. TEREK SANDPIPER *Xenus cinereus* Plates 16, 20.

翹 嘴 鷸

9″. Pale grey, with white trailing edge to wings in flight. Two black stripes form a V on the back in summer. Bright orange legs, rather short. Very long thin slightly upcurved bill (sometimes looks straight). Length of bill is clear distinction from Grey-rumped Sandpiper.

Passage migrant; April, May, September, October.

137. (RED) KNOT *Calidris canutus* **Plates D, 18.**
紅 腹 鷸

10". Plump; similar colouration to Curlew-Sandpiper, but colour of breast not so deep, and shape of bird entirely different; short straight bill, shorter legs, very compact. In flight, shows slight wingbar and greyish rump. Winter plumage is grey above, white below. Forms very compact flocks.

Scarce passage migrant; April, May, September.

138. GREAT KNOT *Calidris tenuirostris* **Plates D, 18.**
薄 嘴 鷸

12". Longish, slightly decurved bill, lack of chestnut on underparts, and broad band of black spots across breast distinguish from Knot in summer. In winter, ashy-grey; at all seasons, white upper tail-coverts are diagnostic in flight.

Passage migrant; April, May, September.

139. EASTERN LITTLE STINT **Plates D, 18.**
(RUFOUS-NECKED STINT)
Calidris ruficollis
紅 脖 鷸

6". Grey-brown and speckled on upperparts; in summer plumage, sides of neck and throat are red, and back is redbrown. Strong black bill. Black legs. Plump and short-necked. One wingbar.

Commonest stint on passage, with some winter records; March to May, August to November.

140. LONG-TOED STINT *Calidris subminuta* **Plate D.**
長 趾 鷸

6". Much browner and more speckled than Eastern Little Stint; yellowish legs. Bill shorter and thinner than Eastern Little Stint. Stance more like a sandpiper than a stint, with longer neck. Prefers grassy areas of marsh, while Eastern Little and Temminck's keep more in the open. One wingbar.

Passage migrant and winter visitor in small numbers, September to May.

141. TEMMINCK'S STINT *Calidris temminckii* **Plate D.**
灰 背 鷸

5½". Almost uniform upperparts, brown in summer, grey in winter, and comparatively short bill, distinguish this from the two preceding species; yellowish legs.

Passage migrant and winter visitor; October to April.

142. SHARP-TAILED SANDPIPER   Plates 15, 18.
Calidris acuminata

尖 尾 鷸

7½". Warm chestnut upperparts, streaked black, and dark streaking on breast and flanks distinguish this from other waders; slight buff superciliary. Spring plumage almost identical with Long-toed Stint, though easily separable by size. Can be confused with Ruff, which is slenderer, with longer legs.

Distinguished from **PECTORAL SANDPIPER Plate 15.** *Calidris melanotos* 7½", by having no abrupt boundary between streaked breast and white underparts; in Pectoral this boundary is sharply defined. Very faint wingbar.

Passage migrant; April, May, September.

143. DUNLIN *Calidris alpina*   Plates 15, 18.

黑 腹 鷸

7". Black belly distinguishes from all other small waders in summer. In winter, slightly decurved bill and greyish breast. One wingbar; blackish centre to rump.

Passage migrant and winter visitor; September to April.

144. CURLEW-SANDPIPER *Calidris ferruginea* Plates 15, 18.

彎 嘴 鷸

7½". In summer, reddish chestnut, deeper and clearer on breast. In winter, safely distinguishable from Dunlin only by white rump in flight, though bill is usually more decurved, and neck and legs appear longer.

Passage migrant; April, May, August, September.

145. SANDERLING *Crocethia alba*   Plates 15, 18.

三 趾 鷸

8". Chestnut upperparts and breast spotted with black in summer; in winter, very pale grey, with conspicuous black patch on carpal joint. Prominent white wingbar; blackish centre to rump.

Scarce passage migrant; April, May, September.

146. SPOON-BILLED SANDPIPER   Plate D.
Eurynorhynchus pygmaeus

匙 嘴 鷸

6". Much like Eastern Little Stint, though paler in winter, and lacking red on neck in summer, and generally more mottled and greyer. Diamond-shaped flattened tip of bill is quite conspicuous, and is the only really diagnostic feature.

Scarce passage migrant; April, May, early October.

147. BROAD-BILLED SANDPIPER   Plates D, 18.
Limicola falcinellus

闊 嘴 鷸

6½". Only slightly larger than stints, with which it associates. Prominent stripe on head, and white eyestripe, are best field-marks, though stripes are less prominent in winter. Long rather thick bill, slightly decurved, often makes the bird look as if it is going to fall forwards. Very dark in flight; no wingbar.

Passage migrant; April, May, September, October.

148. RUFF *Philomachus pugnax*   Plates 15, 18.

流 蘇 鷸

Male 11½", female 9". Mottled grey-brown above, with buff breast; short bill, yellowish legs. In flight, oval white patch either side of tail is diagnostic. Males in summer plumage very variable, with enormous multi-coloured ruff.

Irregular passage migrant; April, September.

PHALAROPES: Phalaropodinae

Small waders, maritime outside breeding season, swim buoyantly; may be seen well out to sea.

149. RED-NECKED PHALAROPE   Plates 16, 18.
Phalaropus lobatus

紅頸瓣蹼鷸

7". Habit of swimming, very high in the water; normally seen in Hong Kong Harbour or on the open sea. Small size, thin bill, gregarious habits are diagnostic. Dark mark through the eye. One white wingbar. Red patch on neck in summer; often seen here in transitional plumage. The only maritime wader here. Very tame.

Irregular passage migrant, sometimes in large numbers; April, May, September.

(GREY PHALAROPE (RED PHALAROPE) *Phalaropus fuli-carius*, 8", though rare on the Asian coast, could occur; dark chestnut underparts in summer plumage are best guide, but thicker bill and lack of striping on back may help to distinguish from Red-necked in winter plumage.)

STILTS and AVOCETS: Recurvirostrinae

Large, black and white waders.

150. BLACK-WINGED STILT Plates 14, 19.
Himantopus himantopus

黑翅長脚鷸

15″. Very long pink legs, projecting beyond tail in flight. Black upperparts, white underparts (male has black crown and back of neck in summer). Needle-like bill.
Passage migrant; April, May, August to November.

151. (PIED) AVOCET *Recurvirostra avosetta* Plates 14, 19.

反 嘴 鷸

17″. Contrasting black and white plumage, upturned bluish bill, and blue legs are unmistakable.
Irregular winter visitor; December to February.

PRATINCOLES: Glareolidae

152. ORIENTAL PRATINCOLE Plates 16, 17.
Glareola maldivarum

燕 鷸

9″. On ground, uniform rich brown, with cream throat-patch, and whitish abdomen. In flight, white abdomen and white upper tail-coverts contrast with brown remainder of plumage; flight graceful and ternlike. Deeply forked tail.
Passage migrant, generally on the Deep Bay Marshes, where it prefers the sandier and dryer areas; also the Airport; April, May, September, October.

GULLS: Larinae

Robust grey and white seabirds (immatures are brown), usually in flocks. Flight with slow wingbeats, powerful and direct.

153. HERRING GULL *Larus argentatus* Plate 21.

銀 鷗

22″. Commonest large gull. Two races, one with pale grey mantle and pink legs, the other with darker mantle and yellow legs; both have black and white tips to primaries; the darker race is not as dark as Slaty-backed, but adults can always be separated safely by the black primaries, noticeably darker than the rest of the wing. Yellow eyering (usually). Bill as Slaty-backed. Immatures brown, with broad dark subterminal bar on tail.
Winter visitor; November to March.

154. COMMON GULL (MEW GULL) *Larus canus* Plate 21.
海 鷗

16″, is like a small Herring Gull of the paler form, with greenish-yellow bill and legs; head lightly streaked in winter.
Two records; January 1968, February 1975.

155. SLATY-BACKED GULL *Larus schistisagus* Plate 21.
黑 灰 背 鷗

24″. Uniform dark slate upperparts are diagnostic of adults. Red eyering. Immatures are much paler than Herring Gulls, almost as pale as Glaucous, but they have a dark subterminal bar on the tail. Pink legs; yellow bill, with red spot on lower mandible.
Rare passage migrant; early April.

156. GLAUCOUS GULL *Larus hyperboreus* Plate 38.
淡 灰 鷗

30″. Large; very pale grey, with primaries even paler; first-year birds are a pale 'milky coffee' colour; second-year birds are almost pure white. Pale primaries are best distinction from **Glaucous-winged Gull** *Larus glaucescens* in adult plumage; immatures of Glaucous-winged are darker than Glaucous, and have primaries uniform with rest of wing (Herring Gull always has darker primaries).
One record, March 1974 (immature; these always wander farthest from breeding range). Due to frequent hybridisation, full field descriptions should be taken of all very pale gulls.

157. GREAT BLACK-HEADED GULL *Larus ichthyaetus*
魚 鷗　　　　　　　　　　　　　　　　　　　　　　　Plate 38.

28″. Very large. Adult has head and throat black in summer, dusky crown in winter; in flight, it has mainly white primaries tipped with black. Immature similar to adult Herring but larger; often has dusky collar; secondaries are white.
One record, December 1974/February 1975.

158. BROWN-HEADED GULL *Larus brunnicephalus*
棕 頭 鷗　　　　　　　　　　　　　　　　　　　　　　Plate 38.

18″. Large white patch at base of primaries is best distinction in winter. Wingtip is black on birds of all ages, with a white spot on adult only. Bill reddish, tipped black; legs orange. Head, throat, and foreneck brown in summer.
Rare winter visitor; several in 1974-75. Probably overlooked previously.

159. BLACK-TAILED GULL *Larus crassirostris*   Plate 21.
黑 尾 鷗

19″. Mantle dark slate. Broad sub-terminal black bar to tail distinguishes adult (some immatures of other species, especially Black-headed, have narrow black sub-terminal bar). Immature dark brown, with almost the whole rear half of the tail darker; bill yellowish tipped red, with a broad black band near the tip, visible at some distance. Legs flesh-coloured.

Winter visitor, particularly in very cold weather (normally immatures); January to March.

160. (COMMON) BLACK-HEADED GULL   Plate 21.
Larus ridibundus

紅 嘴 鷗

15″. In winter plumage, underside of primaries dark grey. White leading edge to wing is best guide; the smallest of the commoner gulls. Legs and bill red.. Dark spot behind eye is all that is left in winter of dark chocolate crown. For differences from Saunders' Gull, see that species.

Common winter visitor; December to March.

161. SAUNDERS' GULL *Larus saundersi*   Plate 21.
黑 嘴 鷗

14″. In winter plumage, distinctions from Black-headed are black patch at base of primaries on otherwise whitish underwing, short black bill (Black-headed has longer reddish bill), and less black on top of primaries. In summer, head is black, not chocolate, with noticeable white eyering; black extends much further down the nape than in Black-headed. Note that Black-headed in summer plumage are rarely, if ever, seen in Hong Kong, whereas some Saunders' Gulls have full summer plumage in late February and early March. No white leading-edge in flight. Tern-like call.

On passage in March, every year since 1969. A few winter.

(KITTIWAKE *Rissa tridactyla*, 16″, distinguished by pure black wingtip and plain grey wings in adult, black bar across back of neck and black 'W' pattern on wings of immature; black legs. One bird in February 1975 was probably of this species, but the Northern Pacific species *R. brevirostris* cannot be entirely ruled out; this species has red legs.)

SKUAS: Stercorariinae

Large brown seabirds, heavily built, and piratical in habits.

162. POMARINE SKUA (POMARINE JAEGER) Plate 21.
Stercorarius pomarinus

扭 尾 海 鷗

20″. Dark brown, with paler patch at base of primaries. Underparts usually pale, with dark breast band, but may be entirely dark. At close range, twisted centre tail feathers extending about 1½″ beyond rest of tail are diagnostic of adult. Best field guide from other skuas is flight, rolling from side to side. Can be expected among flocks of terns, which it forces to disgorge food.

One record; February 1957.

(As other skuas could occur, full field-notes should be taken of any bird seen, noting particularly type of flight, and shape and length of extended central tail-feathers.)

TERNS: Sterninae

Very graceful long-winged sea or marsh birds, with exceptionally buoyant flight.

163. WHITE-WINGED BLACK TERN Plate 22.
(WHITE-WINGED TERN)
Chlidonias leucopterus

黑 海 燕

9¼″. A marsh tern. In summer plumage, black body and wing-linings, white secondaries, upper wing, and tail; bill and legs reddish in summer, blackish in winter. In winter distinguish from Whiskered Tern by white, not grey, rump.

Passage migrant; May, September, October.

(BLACK TERN *Chlidonias niger*, 9½″, a marsh tern; all blackish in summer except for whitish wing-linings, and white under tail-coverts. In winter, similar to Whiskered and White-winged Black, but has blackish patches on sides of breast. The only Hong Kong record of this species, in 1965, does not mention either of the two diagnostic features, and is therefore doubtful; an earlier record is undocumented.)

164. WHISKERED TERN *Chlidonias hybrida* Plate 22.

鬚 海 燕

9¾″. A marsh tern. White cheeks, white wing-linings, and white under tail-coverts distinguish from White-winged Black in summer; in winter, distinguish at close range by grey, not white, rump. Legs and bill dark red in summer, blackish in winter.

Passage migrant; early June, September, October.

Plate 19

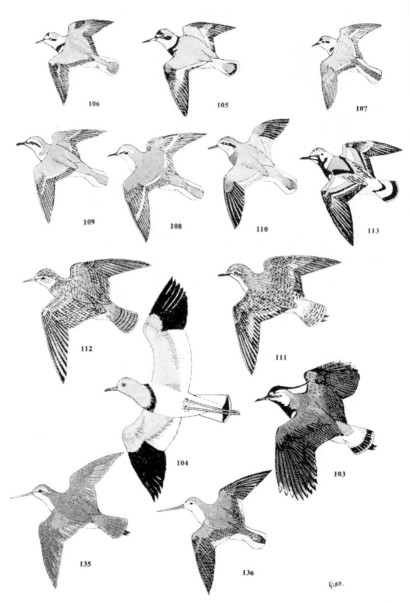

106   105   107

109   108   110   113

112   104   111   103

135   136

Karon

Plate 20

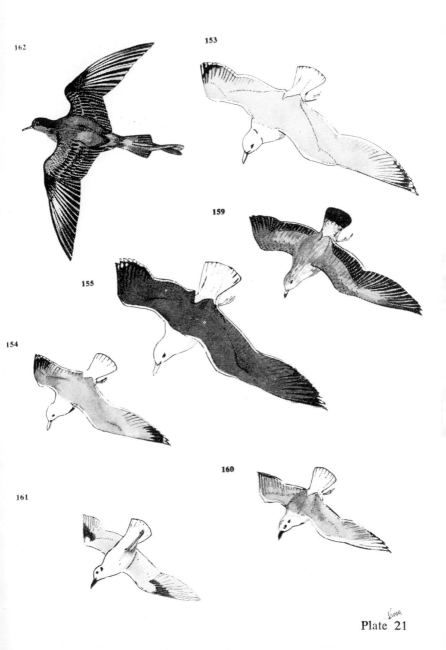

162

153

159

155

154

160

161

Plate 21

163

164

Winter

Summer

Winter

Summer

165

166

170

167

168

169

Plate 22

165. GULL-BILLED TERN *Gelochelidon nilotica*   **Plate 22.**

鷗嘴海燕

15″. Short, stout black bill distinguishes from all other terns. Note comparatively large size. Legs black. Black cap in summer.

Passage migrant; April, May, August, September.

166. CASPIAN TERN *Hydroprogne caspia*   **Plate 22.**

紅嘴巨海燕

21″. Large, almost equal to Herring Gull; heavy bright orange-red bill is visible from a distance. Gull-like in flight. Dark underside of primaries. Black cap in summer.

Passage migrant and winter visitor; recorded in all months of the year, but most frequently in winter.

167. COMMON TERN *Sterna hirundo*   **Plate 22.**

普 通 海 燕

14″. A greyish tern, with white tail and underparts, diagnostic characters being slender black bill at all seasons, and blackish carpal joint (visible at rest and in flight), blackish outer edge to outer rectrices.

Four records; April, June, September.

(Eight records of **ROSEATE TERN** *Sterna dougallii*, 15″, of which none entirely eliminates **ARCTIC TERN** *Sterna paradisaea*. Arctic has red bill, sometimes with black tip; Roseate has primarily black bill, sometimes with red base. Both have longish tail streamers; Roseate has white outer rectrices. Arctic has outer rectrices slightly darker. Both species have red legs. In non-breeding plumage, Arctic and Roseate are probably not safely distinguishable from Common, except by observers with long experience of all three. Roseate is known to migrate down the China coast, but Arctic is a notorious wanderer, so could turn up.)

168. BLACK-NAPED TERN *Sterna sumatrana*   **Plate 22.**

黑 枕 海 燕

13″. Wings and back very pale grey; black line through eye, meeting behind the nape. Remainder white. Legs and bill black. Normally maritime. (If black line is indistinct or fuzzy, take careful field notes and check for **LESSER CRESTED TERN** *Sterna bengalensis*)

Irregular passage migrant; April, May, September, October.

169. LITTLE TERN *Sterna albifrons*   **Plate 22.**
小　海　燕

9½″. Small size, yellow bill with black tip, yellow legs diagnostic. Black cap and white forehead in summer. Appears much smaller than Whiskered and White-winged Black. The only tern which drops to the water almost vertically to feed, though it does not dive.

Passage migrant, usually on the marshes; April, May, September.

170. GREATER CRESTED TERN *Sterna bergii*   **Plate 22.**
大鳳頭海燕

19″. Large. Slight crest. Bill yellow. Not to be confused with very similar **CHINESE CRESTED TERN** *Sterna zimmermanni*, 17″, which is smaller, much paler, and has prominent black tip to yellow bill (Hong Kong record is unacceptable, as it does not mention the black tip).

Three records; May, June, September.

AUKS: Alcidae

Dumpy black, grey, and white seabirds; pointed wings, rapid flight. Dive frequently.

171. ANCIENT AUK *Synthliboramphus antiquus*   **Plate 1.**
海　雀

8″. Grey above, white below, with black head. White stripe behind eye in summer. No wingbar. Caution:— several other similar species could straggle this far south.

One record, May 1975.

PIGEONS and DOVES: Columbidae

Plump, fast-flying woodland birds, with soft crooning calls.

172. BAR-TAILED CUCKOO-DOVE   **Plate E.**
(BARRED CUCKOO-DOVE)
Macropygia unchall

鵑　鳩

15″. Head and neck pinkish-grey; rest of upperparts rich chestnut-brown barred with black; underparts pinkish-grey, with cinnamon patch under tail; bill black; feet red. Female as above, but underparts buffish, barred dark brown. Very long tail. A forest bird.

One record; seen four times, January to April 1960.

173. RUFOUS TURTLE-DOVE   Plate E.
(ORIENTAL TURTLE-DOVE)
Streptopelia orientalis

山 斑 鳩

12″. Distinguish from Spotted Dove by scaly brown appearance of upperparts, and pale grey tips to tail-feathers, as seen from underneath. Black patch on side of neck only, streaked with white.

Passage migrant and winter visitor; September to April.

174. SPOTTED DOVE *Streptopelia chinensis*   Plate E.

珠 頸 斑 鳩

11″. Broad half-collar on sides and back of neck black spotted with white (on Rufous Turtle-Dove, this is smaller, and streaked, not spotted). Upperparts grey-brown, fairly uniform in colouration, underparts pinkish-grey. Tip of tail white underneath, very conspicuous in flight. Flimsy nest of sticks usually about 20 ft. off the ground; March to July.

Abundant resident.

175. RED TURTLE-DOVE   Plate E.
Streptopelia tranquebarica

火 斑 鳩

9″. General colouring reddish-brown; grey head and rump; black collar on hinder part of neck; blackish primaries; lower abdomen pinkish-white; white tip to tail.

Passage migrant, mainly in autumn; September, October.

176. EMERALD DOVE (GREEN-WINGED PIGEON)
Chalcophaps indica   Plate E.

翠 翅 鳩

10″. Bright emerald wings, grey head and belly, white forehead and eyestreak, red bill and legs. A woodland bird, keeping to undergrowth.

Status uncertain, but apparently present throughout the year in Tai Po Kau; one bird captured was apparently not an escape.

(**DOMESTIC PIGEONS,** brown, grey, or white, or a mixture of all three, are descendants of **Rock Doves** *Columba livia*; they are common in the city, and in small flocks in the countryside.)

PARAKEETS: Psittacidae

177. ROSE-RINGED PARAKEET *Psittacula krameri* **Plate E.**

紅領綠鸚鵡

16″. Bright green, with narrow rose-coloured collar; long tail; pointed wings. Flocks readily. Raucous call. Nests in holes; February to May.

Resident, introduced about 1903.

(**SULPHUR-CRESTED COCKATOO** *Cacatua sulphurea,* 13″, can be seen in the city areas; a large white cockatoo with a lemon yellow crest, yellow patch on cheek, and yellow under the tail; raucous and noisy; these are escapees, but may breed, and may have established themselves; the very similar but larger **CITRON-CRESTED COCKATOO** *Cacatua s. citrino-cristata,* 14″, is equally common, and may be distinguished by the orange-yellow, not lemon-yellow, crest.)

CUCKOOS: Cuculidae

Mainly grey, rather hawk-like birds, with longish tails; most species parasitise smaller birds instead of building their own nests.

178. (COMMON) CUCKOO *Cuculus canorus* **Plate E.**

杜　　鵑

12″. Upperparts and throat grey, darker on wings and tail; darker and greyer than Indian Cuckoo; underparts white banded with narrow dark grey bars. Barring on carpal joint. Juveniles and some females reddish-brown, barred blackish. Underside of wing whitish.

Passage migrant; little is known of recent status; April, September, October.

179. HIMALAYAN CUCKOO (ORIENTAL CUCKOO)
　　　　Cuculus saturatus **Plate E.**

中　杜　鵑

11″. Very similar to Cuckoo, but underparts buff with narrow bands of greyish-brown. Pure white patch at carpal joint. Bars on underside usually broader and more widely spaced than Cuckoo. Underside of wing yellowish. Call 'hoo-hoo-hoo'.

Scarce passage migrant; April, October.

180. INDIAN CUCKOO *Cuculus micropterus* **Plate E.**

四　聲　杜　鵑

11″. Dark grey head and neck; upperparts light brownish-grey

—the brownest of species 178-180; chin, throat, and upper breast pale grey; rest of underparts white with broad blackish bars at wide intervals; few bars on under tail-coverts. Call 'one more bottle'. Parasitises most often the Black Drongo.

Summer visitor; April to September.

181. LARGE HAWK-CUCKOO   Plate E.
Cuculus sparverioides

鷹 頭 杜 鵑

13". Head, chin, and throat grey; rest of upperparts dark brown, with bronze sheen, tail barred paler; breast maroon, streaked buff and dark brown; rest of underparts white barred with brown and buff bars set fairly far apart, vent white. Rounded wings. Bill yellow, tipped darker; legs yellow. Most easily found by call, four notes, the last two higher than the first two.

Passage migrant; March, April. Has probably started breeding here in recent years.

182. HODGSON'S HAWK-CUCKOO *Cuculus fugax* Plate E.

棕 腹 杜 鵑

12½". Broad blunt wings are characteristic; grey above, paler below; reddish abdomen; rectrices grey with four dark bars; yellow eyering; the only cuckoo with streaked, not barred, underparts.

One record; October 1971.

183. PLAINTIVE CUCKOO *Cacomantis merulinus*   Plate 23.

八 聲 杜 鵑

9". Head, neck, and breast grey, upperparts brown; underparts wine-red; also has hepatic (red-brown, barred blackish) form, like a small Cuckoo but paler. Plaintive call, ending with a descending trill; repeated constantly, even at night. Parasitises mainly Tailorbirds.

Summer visitor; March to October. Occasional winter records.

184. RED-WINGED CRESTED CUCKOO   Plate 23.
(CHESTNUT-WINGED CUCKOO)
Clamator coromandus

紅翅鳳頭杜鵑

14". Black head and crest; white hind-collar; upperparts black; wings bright chestnut; chin, throat, and upper breast orange chestnut, rest of underparts white; very long tail. Colour-scheme from above suggests Coucal. Secretive.

Four records; April, September, October.

185. DRONGO CUCKOO *Surniculus lugubris* Plate 23.
烏 杜 鵑

10″. Much like a Black Drongo, but outermost rectrix barred white, under tail-coverts barred white, a white bar across underside of primaries and secondaries. Eye brown or crimson; legs and bill black. Behaves like a Cuckoo-Shrike, not a Drongo. Note almost square-ended tail, not deeply forked as Drongo.

One record; May.

186. (COMMON) KOEL *Eudynamis scolopacea* Plate 23.
噪 鵑

14″. Male glossy black, with a deep red eye. Female glossy brown, streaked and spotted with white. Long tail. Male has call 'whee, whee, ou', similar to Great Barbet, but rising on last note; female makes a bubbling note. Parasitises Black-necked Starling, and probably Common and Crested Mynahs.

Resident in thick woods, possibly commoner in summer.

187. CROW-PHEASANT (GREATER COUCAL) Plate 23.
Centropus sinensis
毛 雞

19″. Body and tail black, wings and upper back bright chestnut. Heavy black bill. Long tail. Young birds are duller, the black being spotted and streaked brown. Untidy nest of grass and twigs on the ground; May and June. Call 'boom-boom-boom-boom-boom' increasing in speed, and descending in scale.

Common resident.

188. LESSER CROW-PHEASANT (LESSER COUCAL)
Centropus bengalensis Plate 23.
小 毛 雞

14″. Like small Crow-Pheasant, but back brown, not black, usually with white streaking Call 'boomp-boomp-tocka-tocka-tocka', staccato. Nest as Crow-Pheasant. Resident, not common. Generally prefers higher ground than the Crow-Pheasant.

OWLS: Strigidae

Generally nocturnal raptors, with rounded wings, and pronounced facial disk.

189. (ASIAN) BARRED OWLET   Plate 24.
Glaucidium cuculoides

鵂 鶹

10-11″. Pronounced barring of head and underparts distinguishes this from the two Scops Owls. Largely diurnal. Eyes yellow. A weird bubbling, laughing call.

Former resident, now only occasional.

190. (COMMON) SCOPS OWL *Otus scops*   Plate 24.
紅角貓頭鷹

7½″. Heavily barred and streaked; occurs in two forms, one basically grey, the other basically red-brown. Yellow eyes. Call a loud 'clock-tock-tock'.

Probably a passage migrant; November, December.

191. COLLARED SCOPS OWL *Otus bakkamoena*   Plate 24.
領角貓頭鷹

9½″. Difficult to distinguish from Scops Owl, as both are nocturnal. Eyes are red, brown, or black, never yellow. Call a mournful 'k'waow' repeated at regular intervals for long periods. Nests usually in old Magpie's nest; March to May.

Resident.

192. LONG-EARED OWL *Asio otus*   Plate 24.
長耳貓頭鷹

14″. Note long ear-tufts; yellow eyes. Brown, streaked. Call a moaning 'oo-oo-ooo'. Entirely nocturnal. A species generally of coniferous woodlands.

Two records; March, October.

193. SHORT-EARED OWL *Asio flammeus*   Plate 24.
短耳貓頭鷹

15″. Paler than Long-eared. Hunts in daylight over open country (rolling flight is characteristic); shorter ear-tufts. Dark carpal patch noticeable in flight.

One record; January.

194. BROWN FISH-OWL *Ketupa zeylonensis*   Plate 24.
褐魚貓頭鷹

20″. Very similar to Eagle-Owl, but distinguished by absence of facial disk, and by bare tarsus. Always found near water. Call an eagle-like scream.

Vagrant (used to breed); January to March.

195. BROWN HAWK-OWL *Ninox scutulata*   Plate 24.
褐 鷹 鴞

11″. Dark brown; underparts whitish streaked brown. Facial disk not very noticeable. Longish pointed wings. Long tail distinguishes from all other owls. Largely diurnal. Call 'coo-coo'.

Four records; April, May.

196. (NORTHERN) EAGLE-OWL *Bubo bubo*   Plate 24.
巨 貓 頭 鷹

26-28″. Very large. Prominent ear-tufts. Generally brown, streaked. Whitish throat. Orange eyes. Call a deep 'ooo-hoo', and a guttural grunt or chuckle. Hunts at dawn and dusk. Prefers rocky and craggy areas. Characteristic undulating flight low over ground.

Vagrant.

NIGHTJARS: Caprimulgidae

Nocturnal birds, with long wings, long tails; plumage camouflaged like dead leaves; grey-brown, streaked and spotted with black. Perch lengthwise along branches.

197. JAPANESE NIGHTJAR (GREY NIGHTJAR)   Plate 24.
Caprimulgus indicus

夜   鷹

11″. Male has white bar across first four primaries, white spots on tip of rectrices, conspicuous white gorget; young birds and females usually have buff bar on wings, little white on tail. Call a rapid 'chuck-chuck-chuck-chuck-chuck-chuck'. Nests on ground; April.

Probably resident.

198. SAVANNAH NIGHTJAR *Caprimulgus affinis*
林 夜 鷹

11″. Male has white bar across first two primaries, two to four outer pairs of rectrices white, white gorget; female is paler, with russet-brown wings, no white on tail. Call 'choo-ee' like a whiplash. Nest as Japanese Nightjar.

Probably resident.

SWIFTS: Apodidae

Sickle-shaped wings, short, usually square, tails, weak feet. Rapid flight.

Plate 23

194

196

192

193

195

190

189

191

197

Plate 24

Plate 25

Kevin Phillips

Plate 26

199. LARGE WHITE-RUMPED SWIFT   **Plate F.**
     (FORK-TAILED SWIFT) *Apus pacificus*

白 腰 雨 燕

7″. Plumage as House Swift, but much larger and longer-winged, with deeply-forked tail. Underparts heavily mottled with white, visible at close range. Breeding as House Swift, also on cliffs.

Resident and passage migrant (sometimes large flocks).

200. HOUSE SWIFT *Apus affinis*   **Plate F.**

小白腰雨燕

5″. Blackish-brown, paler on forehead; chin and rump white. Nest generally on beams or ledges inside buildings; May and June.

Resident and passage migrant (sometimes large flocks).

(SPINE-TAILED SWIFT *Hirundapus caudacutus* should occur on passage; 8″; upperparts black, with white spot in centre of back, greyish rump; white chin and throat, breast and abdomen grey, vent white; rectrices spined on the end.)

KINGFISHERS: Alcedinidae

Long heavy bill; pied or brilliant blue; generally near water, except in breeding season. Some species often seen hovering over water and plunging for fish.

201. PIED KINGFISHER *Ceryle rudis*   **Plate 25.**

斑 點 魚 郎

11″. Pied, but far more black and white, less grey, than Crested Kingfisher; also much smaller. Male has two, female one, black band across breast. Hovers frequently. Nests in a deep hole in a river bank; February to April.

Resident in the north-west of the Colony.

202. CRESTED KINGFISHER *Ceryle lugubris*   **Plate 25.**

鳳 頭 魚 郎

15″. Pied, with high black and white crest; some chestnut on breast of male. Male and female both have ill-defined blackish-grey breast-band.

Vagrant, formerly resident.

203. (COMMON) KINGFISHER *Alcedo atthis*   **Plate 25.**

釣 魚 郎

6½ ". Small size, upperparts blue, underparts and stripe through
eye chestnut, white spot on side of cheek; underparts whitish on
young birds. Hovers frequently. Habits as Pied Kingfisher.
Flight low, direct, and very rapid. Nest, a deep hole in a bank,
often some distance from water; April and May.
Resident and passage migrant.

204.WHITE-BREASTED KINGFISHER   **Plate 25.**
     (WHITE-THROATED KINGFISHER)
               Halcyon smyrnensis

白 胸 魚 郎

11". Bright red bill; head, sides of breast, and lower abdomen
chestnut; breast white; upperparts bright blue. White patch on
wings in flight. Does not hover. Nests in holes in banks, not
normally near water; April to June.
Resident and passage migrant.

205. BLACK-CAPPED KINGFISHER   **Plate 25.**
               Halcyon pileata

黑 頭 翁 翠

11". Red bill; black crown, white collar, throat and breast;
lower abdomen bright orange; upperparts deep brilliant violet-
blue. White wing-patch noticeable in flight. Does not hover.
Nesting as White-Breasted.
Scarce resident.

BEE-EATERS: Meropidae

206. BLUE TAILED BEE-EATER   **Plate F.**
               Merops philippinus

栗 喉 蜂 虎

11". Bright bluish-green upperparts; eyestreak black; malar
streak and chin yellow; throat bright chestnut; rest of underparts greenish. Central pair of tail-feathers extend two inches
beyond rest. In flight, very graceful, wings pointed. Bill
decurved. Young birds are paler, bluer, and have little yellow
or chestnut.
Four records; April, May.

ROLLERS: Coraciidae

207. BROAD-BILLED ROLLER (DOLLARBIRD)   Plate 25.
Eurystomus orientalis

三 寶 鳥

9". Bluish green, with brownish head and black tail; highly iridescent, and these colours vary according to the light. Best identified by stocky silhouette and broad flattened red bill, and in flight, round light greenish-blue patches on wings. Normally seen perched on a very exposed branch, or hawking for insects. Passage migrant; April, September to November.

HOOPOES: Upupidae

208. HOOPOE *Upupa epops*   Plate F.

戴　　勝

11". Unmistakable. Plumage and crest cinnamon, crest feathers tipped black; black and white wings and tail. Decurved bill. In flight, wings very broad and rounded, barred black and white. Prefers open grassland. Five records; March, May, August, September, October.

BARBETS: Capitonidae

209. GREAT BARBET *Megalaima virens*   Plate F.

大 擬 啄 木

11". Head bluish-black, nape and upper back brown, wings green glossed crimson; lower back, rump, and tail bright green; underparts green streaked yellow. Vent scarlet. Bill yellow, long, heavy, slightly decurved. Call similar to Koel, but does not rise at the end. Other calls include a rasping croak, and a single note whistled repeatedly. Nests in holes in trees; March to August.
Resident in dense woodland, especially Tai Po Kau and the Lam Tsuen Valley.

WOODPECKERS: Picidae

Sharp-billed wood-boring birds, with stiff tails. Often seen on tree-trunks, when tail acts as a prop. Characteristic drumming sound on wood.

210. BLACK-NAPED GREEN WOODPECKER   Plate 26.
(GREY-HEADED WOODPECKER) *Picus canus*

綠 啄 木 鳥

10". Mainly dark green, with grey head and neck, becoming black on nape. Black eyestripe, black moustache stripe. Male

has crimson forehead. Call, four high metallic notes, all on one tone. Drums frequently in spring. Also has laughing call like the Green Woodpecker of Europe.
Scarce passage migrant; September to March.

211. RUFOUS WOODPECKER   Plate 26.
Micropternus brachyurus

栗 啄 木 鳥

10″. Chestnut-brown, barred and streaked darker. Male has red line below the eye. Loud, laughing call. Eats, and nests in nests of, tree-ants; also nests in holes. Drums, but less frequently than Black-naped.
About eleven records; November to April.

212. (EURASIAN) WRYNECK *Jynx torquilla*   Plate 26.

蚊 鴽

6½″. Grey-brown, heavily vermiculated; grey crown, black eyestripe, continuing down the neck. Behaves like passerine, not like woodpecker. Has habit of twisting its neck at odd angles. Generally in thick scrub or hedges.
Winter visitor; October to March.

PITTAS: Pittidae

213. CHINESE PITTA (BLUE-WINGED PITTA)   Plate F.
Pitta moluccensis

藍翅八色鶇

9″. A ground-haunting bird of thick undergrowth. Crown chestnut, superciliary buff, broad eyestripe black. Rest of upperparts green to turquoise; white patch on primaries; underparts buff, with light scarlet centre of abdomen and vent. Short tail.
Two records; April, July.

LARKS: Alaudidae

214. SMALL SKYLARK (ORIENTAL SKYLARK)   Plate 27.
Alauda gulgula

小 雲 雀

5½″. Upperparts sandy washed rufous, darker on wings. Slight crest. Buff superciliary. Throat pale, breast and flanks reddish-buff streaked brown, abdomen whitish. Legs yellowish-flesh. Distinguish from Richard's Pipit by crest, streaking on breast, and Skylark-like song; colouration is not a good guide, although most Skylarks are darker than most Pipits. Forms flocks in winter. May be conspecific with *Alauda arvensis*.
Scarce resident and winter visitor.

SWALLOWS and MARTINS: Hirundinidae

Streamlined graceful flight; pointed wings; tails more or less forked. Wings are straight, in contrast to sickle-shaped wings of Swifts. Migrate in the daytime, feeding low over the ground as they go.

215. (BARN) SWALLOW *Hirundo rustica*   Plate F.
家　燕

7½". Upperparts blue-black; long tail-streamers with some white at base and tips of feathers; forehead and chin deep red divided by black line from white underparts, tinged reddish. Gregarious on passage. Nests built of mud under eaves of houses; April to June.

Resident, passage migrant, and summer visitor.

216. RED-RUMPED SWALLOW *Hirundo daurica*   Plate F.
金　腰　燕

7". Like Swallow, but rump, throat, and whole of underparts reddish-buff; tail-streamers not usually so long. Gregarious on passage.

Passage migrant; April, October, November.

217. (COMMON) HOUSE MARTIN   Plate F.
     Delichon urbica

毛　脚　燕

5". Black, with white rump and underparts; tail short and forked. Often over water while feeding.

Scarce passage migrant; March, October.

218. SAND MARTIN *Riparia riparia*   Plate F.
沙　燕

4¾". Brown upperparts and gorget, white chin and under-parts. Short tail slightly forked. Flocks. Feeds usually over water.

Passage migrant; April, May, September, October.

SHRIKES: Laniidae

Perch on exposed perches, watching for their prey. In adult plumage, all have a prominent black eyestripe. Bill thick and slightly hooked. Rather long tail. Call-notes harsh.

219. CHINESE (GREAT) GREY SHRIKE   Plate 28.
Lanius sphenocercus

楔 尾 伯 勞

11-13″. Pale grey upperparts with black eyestripe and primaries, white superciliary, and a prominent white patch on the wing. Underparts white. Central rectrices black tipped with white; outer rectrices white. Catches food in mid-air, or pounces from above; hovers frequently.

Two records; November.

220. RUFOUS-BACKED SHRIKE   Plate 28.
(LONG-TAILED SHRIKE)
Lanius schach

棕 背 伯 勞

9½″. Long tail, and habit of perching on telegraph wires are distinctive. Crown grey, eyestripe black; upperparts chestnut with grey to black wings; underparts white shading to rufous on flanks and vent. A wholly or partly melanistic form is not uncommon. Call loud and harsh, but it also imitates other species. Nests in bushes about ten feet off the ground; March to June.

Resident, perhaps with greater numbers in summer.

221. BULL-HEADED SHRIKE *Lanius bucephalus*   Plate 28.
牛 頭 伯 勞

7½″. Chestnut crown, narrow white superciliary, grey-brown wings, and white spot on wing distinguish adult male; underparts buffish, mottled on breast and flanks, paler on centre of throat and centre of abdomen, but never white. Female has whole of underparts buffish-chestnut, with scalloping down the flanks.

222. TIGER SHRIKE *Lanius tigrinus*   Plate 28.
虎 紋 伯 勞

7½″. Male has grey crown and neck, no superciliary; wings deep chestnut, conspicuously barred paler; underparts white, tinged buff. Female has white down centre of underparts, scalloping on flanks; slight white superciliary. Only shrike with barred upperparts in all plumages. Noticeably thick bill.

One specimen; February (1908, Vaughan and Jones); the specimen is lost, so the record cannot be taken as certain.

223. BROWN SHRIKE *Lanius cristatus*   Plate 28.
紅 尾 伯 勞

7″. Crown chestnut or grey; white superciliary; chestnut-brown wings; white spot on carpal joint of some; throat white in all plumages (buff in Bull-headed Shrike). Rest of underparts whitish, with grey or buff markings on breast and flanks. Juveniles barred above and below. Very variable, as several subspecies may be involved.

Passage migrant and winter visitor; September to May.

ORIOLES: Oriolidae

224. BLACK-NAPED ORIOLE *Oriolus chinensis*   Plate 26.
黑 枕 黃 鸝

10". Adults are bright yellow, with a black eyestripe meeting at the back of the crown. Primaries and centre of tail black. Females and young birds are greenish-yellow, more or less streaked. Keeps to tops of trees. Musical 'wheel-a-wee-oo' and similar flute-like calls draw attention to the bird. Nest a deep cup slung in the fork of a branch, made of grass, moss, etc.; April to June.

Summer visitor, with occasional winter records; April to October.

DRONGOS: Dicruridae

Slender black or grey birds with long forked tails. Grating call-notes. Catch insect prey by darting out from a branch to seize it in mid-air. Normally on prominent perches. Often nest in loose colonies.

225. BLACK DRONGO   Plate 26.
Dicrurus macrocercus (syn. *adsimilis*)

黑 捲 尾

10". Black with blue sheen; tail deeply forked, but does not curl upwards. Call like a creaking gate. A bird of open country. Nest built of grass at the end of a high bough; April to June.

Summer visitor, but a few winter; March to October.

226. ASHY DRONGO *Dicrurus leucophaeus*   Plate 26.
灰 捲 尾

11½". Grey, with deeply forked tail; two forms occur in Hong Kong, of which one, subspecies *leucogenis*, has conspicuous white cheek-patch.

Passage migrant and winter visitor; October to March.

227. HAIR-CRESTED DRONGO   Plate 26.
    (SPANGLED DRONGO) *Dicrurus hottentottus*

髮 冠 捲 尾

11½ ". As Black Drongo, but outer tail-feathers curl noticeably outwards or upwards; tail only slightly forked. Sheen is
green rather than blue. A crest of narrow feathers curls back
from the forehead. Noisy and aggressive, mobbing any bird of
prey. In display-flight, rises to a peak, then plunges down with
wings half closed. A bird of the forest. Nest as Black Drongo.
Summer visitor, occasional in winter; March to October.

STARLINGS: Sturnidae

Stocky birds with long pointed bills, short tails. All species are
gregarious. Generally in scrub country and small woods.

228. CHINESE STARLING   Plate 28.
    (WHITE-SHOULDERED STARLING) *Sturnus sinensis*

噪 林 鳥

7". Grey, with black wings, whitish rump, whitish underparts,
black tail tipped white. Diagnostic feature is large white patch
on wings of male; small size. No black on head. Bill blue,
legs greyish. Nests in crevices of buildings and holes in trees;
May.

Present throughout the year.

229. SILKY STARLING (RED-BILLED STARLING)
     Sturnus sericeus   Plate 28.

絲 光 椋 鳥

8½ ". Grey, with black wings and tail, and a small white wing-
patch; rump paler, but not white. Distinguish from Grey
Starling by uniform grey head, and faint, but distinct, brownish
collar. Female duller. Bill crimson tipped black, legs orange.
Winter visitor; October to March.

230. GREY STARLING   Plate 28.
    (WHITE-CHEEKED STARLING) *Sturnus cineraceus*

灰 椋 鳥

8½ ". Distinguish from very similar Silky Starling by dark
crown, white forehead and cheeks; breast usually blackish; white
band across rump. Head of female more streaked. Generally

PLATE A

PLATE B

PLATE C

PLATE D

PLATE E

PLATE F

PLATE G

PLATE H

a much browner bird than Silky or Chinese. Bill orange tipped black, legs orange.
Winter visitor; October to March.

230a. CHESTNUT-CHEEKED STARLING   Plate 38.
Sturnus philippensis
小 椋 鳥
6½ ". A small dark starling, possibly conspecific with Purple-backed. Plumage very variable, but diagnostic features are reddish-chestnut patch on sides of neck, white wingbar, and white rump. Upperparts mainly grey, almost black on back and tail, and dark brown on primaries; underparts pale grey to white.
One record,. March 1976.
(PURPLE-BACKED STARLING *Sturnus sturninus*, 7", is similar to Chinese, but has metallic purple back and spot on nape; messy double white wingbar at rest (conspicuous from underneath in flight). No white on tail. Immatures are duller, browner. Could occur.)

231. COMMON STARLING *Sturnus vulgaris*   Plate 28.
紫 翅 椋 鳥
8½ ". Blackish-brown, browner on young birds, heavily speckled with paler brown in winter. Purple sheen. Gregarious; associates with other starlings.
A small flock has wintered annually at Lokmachau since 1971-72; November to March.

232. BLACK-NECKED STARLING   Plate 28.
(BLACK-COLLARED STARLING)
Sturnus nigricollis
黑 領 椋 鳥
11". White head; neck and upper breast black, forming a collar. Rest of upperparts dark brown, with white wingpatch and rump; underparts white. Call a harsh whistle. Large untidy domed nest high up in a tree; April to August.
Resident in the north of the New Territories.

233. COMMON MYNAH *Acridotheres tristis*   Plate 28.
家 八 哥
10". Head, neck, and upper breast black, rest chocolate brown; vent whitish. White patch at base of outer primaries and white tips to rectrices visible in flight. Bill, legs, and fleshy wattle yellow. Nest as Crested Mynah.
Introduced species, now mainly confined to the Mong Tseng Peninsula.

234. CRESTED MYNAH *Acridotheres cristatellus* **Plate 28.**

八 哥

9½ ". Black, with white wingpatch and tips to rectrices. Prominent tuft of black feathers just above bill. Bill and legs yellow. Nests in hole, or old nest of other species; April to July.

Common resident.

(**HILL MYNAH** *Gracula religiosa* is a common cage-bird, and escapes are often seen; very similar to Common Mynah, but black instead of brown; wattle bright yellow.)

CROWS: Corvidae

Large birds with powerful bills; primarily woodland species.

235. (EURASIAN) JAY *Garrulus glandarius* **Plate 29.**

松 鴉

13". Pinkish-brown; white rump; black tail; wings barred black, white, and blue. Noisy. Call a raucous 'skraaak'. Often in small parties; in thick woodland.

Scarce winter visitor, possibly resident; October to April.

236. BLUE MAGPIE *Urocissa erythrorhyncha* **Plate 29.**

藍 喜 鵲

21". Bluish-grey, with white on nape, tips of wing-coverts, in bars along rectrices, and belly. Very long tail (14-15") curves downwards at tip. Red bill and legs. A wide variety of calls, often imitative. Usually in small parties in woodland. Nest built of twigs in thick undergrowth; April to July.

Resident.

237. (BLACK-BILLED) MAGPIE *Pica pica* **Plate 29.**

喜 鵲

18". Unmistakable glossy black and white plumage and long graduated tail. The commonest large bird of open country, often in small parties; very noisy (a loud, quick, 'chak-chak-chak-chak', etc.). Nest a large domed affair of sticks generally high in a tree; February to May.

Resident.

238. (GREY) TREEPIE *Dendrocitta formosae* **Plate 29.**

灰 樹 鵲

11-13". Forehead, lores, and cheeks black; crown and upper back slate; rest of upperparts rufous; whitish patch on wing. Whitish rump conspicuous in flight. Underparts greyish with chestnut vent. A range of harsh calls. Keeps to thick woodland. Gregarious.

Irregular winter visitor; irruptions; December to March.

(**ROOK** *Corvus frugilegus*, 18″, black, with strong grey bill. Two Hong Kong records, both without field-notes.)

239. JUNGLE CROW (LARGE-BILLED CROW)   Plate 29.
Corvus macrorhynchus

大 嘴 烏 鴉

21″. Large, entirely black, including powerful bill. Call a harsh croak. Usually in pairs or small parties. Nest built of sticks high up in a tree; March to June.

Resident.

240. COLLARED CROW *Corvus torquatus*   Plate 29.

白 頸 鴉

18″. Black, except for very conspicuous white hind-collar and bib. Usually in pairs. Nest and voice as Jungle Crow; December to April.

Resident, probably restricted to the north and east of the New Territories, and Stonecutters' Island.

CUCKOO-SHRIKES and MINIVETS: Campephagidae

Slim active birds of the canopy; Cuckoo-Shrikes generally solitary; Minivets generally in flocks. Cuckoo-Shrikes have rounded wings, Minivets pointed wings.

241. BLACK-WINGED CUCKOO-SHRIKE   Plate 26.
Coracina melaschistos

暗 灰 鵑 鵙

8½″. A grey bird with dark wings; lores dark; white barring under tail. In general appearance similar to Ashy Drongo, but behaviour different; Cuckoo-Shrike finds its food among the upper branches and leaves, does not hawk for flies. Female paler.

242. GREATER CUCKOO-SHRIKE   Plate 26.
(LARGE CUCKOO-SHRIKE) *Coracina novae-hollandiae*

大 鵑 鵙

12″. Much larger and darker than the Black-winged Cuckoo-Shrike; sides of head black; throat blackish on male. Abdomen and under tail-coverts white, but no white barring on tail.

One record; November.

243. ROSY MINIVET *Pericrocotus roseus*
粉紅山椒鳥

7", is possibly conspecific with Ashy Minivet, but is supposedly distinguishable from it by pale brown rump, dark brown wings, and lack of black eyestripe; note that it has black lores.
One record, March.

244. ASHY MINIVET *Pericrocotus divaricatus*   Plate 29.
灰 山 椒 鳥

7". Grey, with black eyestripe, white forehead, cheeks, and chin; wing black, with white bar, and white patch at carpal joint; most of outer rectrices white; central rectrices and base of outer, black; underparts white. Usually in small parties, very active, moving from bush to bush, calling constantly.
Passage migrant; March, April, September, October.

245. GREY-THROATED MINIVET   Plate 29.
(GREY-CHINNED MINIVET) *Pericrocotus solaris*
灰喉山椒鳥

7". Like a small Scarlet Minivet, but male is flame-red, not scarlet, has greyish throat-patch, and only one bar on wing; head is grey instead of black. Female has whitish throat-patch, no yellow on forehead. Wingbar of male is largely yellow in flight. Prefers to keep to tops of trees.
Six records; November to March.

246. SCARLET MINIVET *Pericrocotus flammeus*   Plate 29.
紅赤山椒鳥

8". Male brilliant scarlet and black; head, neck, most of upperparts and wing black; rump, outer pairs of rectrices, double wingbar, and underparts scarlet; vent white. Females and juveniles have yellow in place of scarlet, yellowish-olive in place of black of upperparts; wings blackish with yellow wingbars; grey crown and eyestripe. In spring, young males are orange instead of yellow. Usually in parties (adult males perhaps one in fifteen birds).
Irregular winter visitor; December to March.

BULBULS: Pycnonotidae

Noisy, medium-sized birds of scrubland and woodlands; gregarious.

247. CHESTNUT BULBUL *Hypsipetes castanotus*   **Plate 30.**
栗背短脚鵯
7½". Chestnut forehead, sides of head, and upperparts; crown
blackish chestnut. Wings and tail brown. Throat white, breast
greyish, underparts white. More often heard than seen, as it
keeps to thick woodland; call 'ting-a-ling' like a bicycle bell.
Irregular winter visitor, normally only in Tai Po Kau; irruptions; November to April.

248. BLACK BULBUL   **Plate 30.**
        Hypsipetes madagascariensis
黑 短 脚 鵯
8½". Black; complete head is white in adult, but in most birds
it is a mixture of black and white. Bill and legs bright red
in adult, blackish in young. Call plaintive, like a cat mewing,
but harsher.
Irregular winter visitor, normally only in Tai Po Kau; irruptions; January to March.

249. CRESTED BULBUL   **Plate 30.**
    (RED-WHISKERED BULBUL) *Pycnonotus jocosus*
高 雞 冠
7½". Prominent black crest, white cheeks, red whiskers and
vent; otherwise brown above, white below; rectrices tipped white.
Nest a cup built of grasses, generally in a thick bush; April to
June.
Very common resident.

250. CHINESE BULBUL   **Plate 30.**
    (LIGHT-VENTED BULBUL) *Pycnonotus sinensis*
白 頭 翁
6½". A greenish-brown bird with forehead and crown black,
nape, chin, and throat white; black stripe from base of bill
running below the eye to meet across the nape; underparts
white, greyish on breast. Immatures have greyish heads, with
only a trace of adult pattern. Nest as Crested Bulbul.
Very common resident, forming large flocks in winter.

251. RED-VENTED BULBUL   **Plate 30.**
    (SOOTY-HEADED BULBUL) *Pycnonotus aurigaster*
紅 屎 忽
8½". Black fore-crown; rest of upperparts brown, with white
tips to rectrices; underparts pale brown, with red vent. Pale
rump noticeable in flight. Nest as Crested.

Common resident, generally preferring higher elevations than Crested and Chinese.

(FINCH-BILLED BULBUL (COLLARED FINCHBILL) *Spizixos semitorques*, 6½″; head and nape black to dark grey; white gorget, and a few streaks on ear-coverts; rest of upperparts and breast green, with some yellow marking; abdomen greenish-yellow; under tail-coverts bright yellow; black subterminal band on tail. One record, April 1974, probably an escape.)

(ORANGE-BELLIED LEAFBIRD *Chloropsis hardwickii*, 7″, is green, with deep purple breast, wings and tail, black chin, throat, and sides of head, orange abdomen; female almost entirely green; one record and a possible second; a common cage-bird, and therefore records are suspect, as it is normally a montane species.)

BABBLERS: Timaliinae

A varied family of mainly ground and undergrowth haunting birds, usually brown, with a wide variety of calls.

252. BLACK-FACED LAUGHING-THRUSH   **Plate 36.**
     (MASKED LAUGHING-THRUSH)
         Garrulax perspicillatus

七　姊　妹

12″. Brown above, whitish below; black cheeks; rufous vent. Travels through undergrowth in small parties, with a noisy chattering. Nests in thick bushes up to twenty feet from the ground; March to August.
Common resident.

253. BLACK-THROATED LAUGHING-THRUSH   **Plate 36.**
         Garrulax chinensis

黑　喉　噪　鶥

10½″. Crown grey, back olive-brown, darker on wings. Forehead, eyering and stripe behind eye, chin, and centre of throat black; cheeks white; breast grey, underparts whitish. Characteristic flute-like song. Skulking. Nesting as Black-faced Laughing-Thrush.
Resident on Hong Kong Island.

254. HWAMEI *Garrulax canorus*   **Plate 36.**

畫　眉

9″. Rich golden-brown above and below, streaked darker above and on breast; white ring round eye and short stripe behind eye. Skulking; good song; chattering call-notes. Nests in low bushes; April to July.

Common on Hong Kong Island; local in the New Territories.
(WHITE-CHEEKED LAUGHING-THRUSH (WHITE-BROWED
LAUGHING-THRUSH) *Garrulax sannio*, 9½", brown above
and below, with white lores, cheeks, superciliary, and abdomen;
eyering and stripe behind eye dark brown; quieter, more skulking than Black-faced Laughing-Thrush; may occur, but published
records are either undated, or otherwise unsubstantiated, or in
localities where escapes are likely; may be breeding ferally on
Hong Kong Island.)

255. GREATER NECKLACED LAUGHING-THRUSH
Garrulax pectoralis **Plate 36.**

黑 領 噪 鶥

11-12". Upperparts bright chestnut, with greenish tinge on
back; subterminal black band on tail; tips of rectrices pale.
Lores, eyering, and superciliary white; post-orbital stripe curving
down the neck and across to meet in the middle of the breast,
black; ear-coverts white spotted black; line from eyering below
ear-coverts to join post-orbital stripe, black; flanks and vent
rufous; rest of underparts white. Typical Laughing-Thrush
series of calls. Gregarious.

Winter visitor to Tai Po Kau, possibly now resident; October to
April.

(LESSER NECKLACED LAUGHING-THRUSH *Garrulax
monileger* differs from *G. pectoralis* in having black lores, and
no black line below mainly white ear-coverts; outer rectrices
spotted black and white; no records.)

(RUFOUS-NECKED SCIMITAR-BABBLER (STREAK-BREAST-
ED SCIMITAR-BABBLER) *Pomatorhinus ruficollis*, 6½", upperparts chestnut; long white superciliary; lores, ear-coverts, and
upper cheeks black; sides of neck bright chestnut; throat white;
breast white, spotted chestnut; abdomen white tinged chestnut;
bill slightly decurved. A skulking bird of the undergrowth,
normally travelling in pairs. A record for 1949 has no details
or precise date, and is therefore unsubstantiated.)

256. CHINESE BABAX *Babax lanceolatus* **Plate 36.**

矛 紋 草 鶥

10". Dark chestnut brown, feathers edged paler, giving streaked
appearance; wings and tail dull brown; sides of head whitish,
with dark moustache patch; underparts cream, streaked chestnut
on breast and flanks. Bill long, black, decurved. A montane
species. Nests in low bushes; June.

Apparently resident on Tai Mo Shan 1959-63, but not seen there
since.

(PEKIN ROBIN (RED-BILLED LEIOTHRIX) *Leiothrix lutea*, 5½". Yellowish olive crown shading to greyish-olive back; primaries blackish with a crimson patch at their base, and a golden patch above that. Tail deeply forked. Bill red. Face yellowish-white with greyish moustache-stripe; golden throat; orange breast; white abdomen; yellow vent. This species is so common as a cagebird that many records are undoubtedly of escapes; some may be of genuinely wild birds, but most recent records are from Hong Kong Island, which tends to suggest that they are escapes; it is a montane species.)

(LESSER SCALY-BREASTED WREN-BABBLER (PYGMY WREN-BABBLER) *Pnoepyga pusilla*, 3"; upperparts golden-brown, underparts whitish, each feather edged brown, and with black centre; practically no tail. The only published record is without description.)

257. COLLARED SIVA (STRIATED YUHINA)   Plate 34.
Yuhina castaniceps

栗 頭 希 鶥

5½". Greyish crown and crest; brown cheeks, sides of neck, and nape; with white streaking on sides of neck; upperparts olive-brown, underparts white, brownish on flanks and vent. Gregarious. Tit-like behaviour. Persistent chattering calls.

Irregular winter visitor; single records of flocks in January and December 1966; quite widespread October 1973 to March 1974. Again 1975-6.

258. WHITE-BELLIED YUHINA   Plate 34.
Yuhina zantholeuca

白 腹 鳳 鶥

4½". Upperparts bright yellowish-green; conspicuous crest; lores whitish, cheeks and ear-coverts grey grading to yellowish-green; chin and centre of underparts whitish, rest of underparts pale grey; vent yellow. Long, pointed, decurved pink bill. Tit-like behaviour.

Recorded in autumn 1953 only; August to October.

PANURIDAE: Parrotbills

(VINOUS-THROATED PARROTBILL *Paradoxornis webbianus*, 5"; rufous head and neck, rufous-brown upperparts, brighter on wing, duller on tail; cheeks, throat, and breast vinous-brown, pale, grading into buffish abdomen; stubby parrot-like bill. Normally a montane species. Recorded at least twice from the University area, notorious for its long list of escapes.)

214

331

329

328

330

332

333

335

334

335

337

337

336

337

Plate 27

Plate 28

Plate 29

Plate 30

PARADISE FLYCATCHERS: Monarchinae

Forest flycatchers, keeping to undergrowth of thick woodland.

259. INCE'S PARADISE FLYCATCHER   Plate 33.
(ASIAN PARADISE FLYCATCHER)
Terpsiphone paradisi

壽 帶 鳥

8″, of which half is tail. Very similar to the Japanese Paradise
Flycatcher, but distinguished by eyering, blue in summer, black
in winter, and chestnut, not maroon, gloss on upperparts; chestnut tail. Female has shorter tail.
Passage migrant; April, October.

260. JAPANESE PARADISE FLYCATCHER   Plate 33.
Terpsiphone atrocaudata

紫 壽 帶 鳥

8″, of which half is tail. Head, neck, and breast black, with
pronounced crest; remainder dark chestnut, glossed maroon.
Lower breast grey, grading to white on abdomen. Tail black.
Female has dark brown, and shorter, tail. Blue eyering.
Scarce passage migrant; April, October.

261. GREY-HEADED FLYCATCHER   Plate 33.
Culicicapa ceylonensis

方 尾 鶲

5″. Head, neck and upper breast grey; white eyering. Upper-
parts bright yellowish-green; underparts clear yellow.
Passage migrant and occasional winter visitor; November to
March.

262. BLACK-NAPED MONARCH FLYCATCHER   Plate 33.
(BLACK-NAPED MONARCH)   *Hypothymis azurea*

黑 枕 王 鶲

6″. Male blue, with black patch on nape, black band around
base of throat, and black at base of bill; breast blue fading
into whitish abdomen. Female lacks the black, and has brown
upperparts, washed blue; immatures have brown wings, washed
blue.
Passage migrant and winter visitor; November to March.

FLYCATCHERS: Muscicapinae

Plump, alert little birds which hawk for flies in woodlands; often
return to the same perch after sallying forth after a fly.

263. (ASIAN) BROWN FLYCATCHER   Plate 33.
Muscicapa latirostris

闊 嘴 鶲

5″. Brownish-grey above, white below; whitish eyering; slight white barring on wing. At close range. breast and flanks are very pale grey. Usually the commonest flycatcher in woodlands; generally keeps just below the canopy.
Passage migrant and winter visitor; September to April.

264. GREY-SPOTTED FLYCATCHER   Plate 33.
(GREY-STREAKED FLYCATCHER)
Muscicapa griseisticta

斑 胸 鶲

5½″. A grey-brown bird, somewhat streaked on upperparts, with white throat and eyering, and conspicuous streaking on breast and flanks. Rest of underparts white. Usually selects the most exposed perch possible.
Passage migrant; April, May, October, November.

265. SOOTY FLYCATCHER (DARK-SIDED FLYCATCHER)
Muscicapa sibirica   Plate 38.

烏 鶲

5″. Similar to Brown and Grey-spotted, but distinguished by dark grey patches on breast, making the whole underparts look dark. Chooses exposed perches as Grey-spotted, and has distinctive triangular appearance when perched (caused by wingtips almost meeting end of tail). Generally darker brown than either Brown or Grey-spotted.
One record, October 1974.

266. FERRUGINOUS FLYCATCHER   Plate 34.
Muscicapa ferruginea

紅 褐 鶲

4½″. Dark grey head; lores, eyering, cheeks, and centre of underparts white; upperparts rusty, brighter on rump and tail; flanks and vent bright chestnut-orange; female duller and paler.
Irregular passage migrant, only in spring; April.

267. VERDITER FLYCATCHER *Muscicapa thalassina*
銅 藍 鶲   Plate 34.

6″. Greenish-blue, with a black patch in front of the eye; female duller; the only all-blue flycatcher, though colour can look green in some lights. Prefers tops of trees, telegraph wires.
Winter visitor; October to March.

268. RED-BREASTED FLYCATCHER   **Plate 33.**
(RED-THROATED FLYCATCHER)   *Ficedula parva*

紅　喉　鶲

4½ ". A plump brown flycatcher usually characterised by conspicuous white patches on outer rectrices; tail otherwise black. Male has red breast in spring. Habit of flicking its tail open, showing the white, is good guide, but some birds have little white on tail, and must be recognised by uniform colouring of upperparts, shape, and tail-flicking. Posture horizontal rather than upright. Keeps fairly close to the ground, often along hedges or bunds.

Passage migrant and winter visitor; October to April.

269. ROBIN FLYCATCHER   **Plate 33.**
(MUGIMAKI FLYCATCHER)   *Ficedula mugimaki*

鴝　鶲

4½-5". Male black, with short white eyestripe and wingbar; underparts chestnut-red on breast, yellow on abdomen. Female and immatures, olive-brown, with white spot on carpal joint; underparts white, tinged reddish on breast. Plumage in winter very variable, and males may show anything between the two types of plumage described. Often in small flocks. Feeds in treetops as well as near ground.

Passage migrant and winter visitor; October to April.

270. NARCISSUS FLYCATCHER   **Plate 33.**
Ficedula narcissina

黑背黃眉鶲

5". Male as Tricolour Flycatcher, but eyebrow golden instead of white; breast more orange. Female is olive, with pale eyering, olive-green rump, some rufous on tail; underparts cream, washed brown. Generally in undergrowth.

Passage migrant, recorded only in spring; April.

271. TRICOLOUR FLYCATCHER   **Plate 33.**
(YELLOW-RUMPED FLYCATCHER)
Ficedula zanthopygia

白　眉　鶲

4½ ". Male with black upperparts, white eyebrow and wingbar, golden rump and underparts. Female is olive, with whitish wingbar, golden rump, and pale yellow underparts. Generally in undergrowth.

Scarce passage migrant, generally in autumn; April, September.

272. HAINAN BLUE FLYCATCHER Plate 34.
Cyornis hainana

海南藍鶲

5½″. Male like small edition of Blue and White, but black of breast fades gradually into white underparts. No white on tail. Female olive-brown, with chestnut-buff chin and throat. The skulking habits of this species make confusion with Blue and White unlikely.

Occasional visitor; has bred.

273. BLUE AND WHITE FLYCATCHER Plate 34.
Cyanoptila cyanomelana

白腹藍鶲

6″. Male blue above, darker on wings; sides of head and upper breast black, clearly demarcated from white underparts; white bar near base of tail visible in flight. Female is olive-brown above, chin and breast olive washed rusty, bluish wash on wings and tail; abdomen white washed rusty, vent white. Male generally makes itself rather conspicuous, but female rarely seen. Passage migrant, males common; March, April, September, October.

(BLUE-THROATED FLYCATCHER *Cyornis rubeculoides*, 5″, skulking; male has blue above and on chin and upper throat; rest of underparts orange; distinguishable from TICKELL'S BLUE FLYCATCHER *Cyornis tickelliae* only by amount of blue on throat, as Tickell's has only a trace of blue; a bird which wintered 1968-69 was probably Blue-throated, but Tickell's cannot be entirely eliminated.)

(RUFOUS-BELLIED NILTAVA *Niltava sundara/davidi*, 6½″, male has upperparts and throat blue, with chestnut shafts to primaries; underparts orange, fading to yellow on vent; female is brown above, pale brown below, with blue spot on side of neck, and white gorget. The two species are probably indistinguishable in the field; sight records in 1968 and 1973 could refer to either.)

WARBLERS: Sylviinae

A very large family of insectivorous birds, with slender bills; mainly dull-coloured and small. Many are difficult to identify, and *Phylloscopus* warblers in particular should be treated with great caution.

274. CHINESE BUSH-WARBLER   Plate 30.
(JAPANESE BUSH-WARBLER)   *Cettia diphone*

短翅樹鶯

6½" male, 5" female. Russet brown, with buffish superciliary; underparts dirty white. White of under wing-coverts shows in front of carpal joint when wing is closed. Distinguished by comparatively large size (of male), general brown colouring, habit of feeding in undergrowth, or bushes shaded by larger trees. Churring alarm calls; spring song 'wichiti, wichiti, weela, we-oo'.

Winter visitor; October to March.

275. SHORT-TAILED BUSH-WARBLER   Plate 30.
(STUB-TAILED BUSH-WARBLER)
Cettia squameiceps

鱗頭樹鶯

4". Dark brown, mottled, with a long buffish-white superciliary, very short tail; underparts pale brown. Creeps around among dead leaves on the forest floor. Call a sharp 'tuck-tuck-tuck'. Can only be confused with Wren, q.v.

Winter visitor; November to March.

276. MOUNTAIN BUSH-WARBLER
(BROWNISH-FLANKED BUSH-WARBLER)
Cettia fortipes

山 樹 鶯

4½-5". Very similar to female Chinese Bush-Warbler, but latter should show a little white on carpal joint and under wing-coverts. Call a harsh 'chack'. Behaviour as Chinese Bush-Warbler.

Four records; possibly confused with Chinese Bush-Warbler; September to January.

277. PALLAS'S GRASSHOPPER WARBLER   Plate 31.
(PALLAS'S WARBLER)   *Locustella certhiola*

小 蝗 鶯

4½-5". A bird of reedbeds. Upperparts brown, streaked black, with buff eyebrow; underparts whitish; pale brown on flanks. Some streaking on breast of immature. Rufous rump and upper tail-coverts. Distinguish from Fantail Warbler by longer tail, very little streaking on crown. Skulking.

Scarce passage migrant; April, September, October.

(GRAY'S GRASSHOPPER WARBLER *Locustella fasciolata*, 6", unstreaked brown upperparts, underparts suffused with buff:

breast greyish; slight white superciliary. Young birds have pale yellow underparts. Tail noticeably rounded; haunts dense thickets. Slimmer bill and rounded tail are best distinctions from Styan's Grasshopper Warbler. Could occur on migration.)

(**LANCEOLATED WARBLER** *Locustella lanceolata*, 4½ ", very smilar to Pallas's Grasshopper Warbler, but has streaked breast and flanks in all plumages; rump the same colour as rest of upperparts. Runs along the ground. Could occur in winter or on migration.)

278. STYAN'S GRASSHOPPER WARBLER   Plate 31.
Locustella pleskei

伊豆島蝗鶯

5½ ". Brown, unstreaked, with greyish-buff eyebrow; underparts whitish. Heavy Reed-Warbler-like bill. Found among reeds. The only recorded species with similar plumage is the Great Reed-Warbler, which is much larger.

Passage migrant (specific status of this form is uncertain, but as bill is much larger, and wing-formula and song differ from *L. certhiola* and *L. ochotensis*, it seems likely to be a separate species); April, September, October.

(**MIDDENDORFF'S (GRASSHOPPER) WARBLER** *Locustella ochotensis*, 5½ ", similar in the field to Styan's Grasshopper Warbler, but with slimmer bill, and some mottling on the upperparts. Could occur on migration.)

279. VON SCHRENCK'S REED-WARBLER   Plate 31.
(BLACK-BROWED REED-WARBLER)
Acrocephalus bistrigiceps

黑眉葦鶯

5 ". Brown above, unstreaked, with pale chestnut rump. Buff eyebrow stripe, with black stripe above it. Yellowish eyering; dark post-orbital stripe. Underparts buffish, whiter on throat. In reedbeds. Tuneless rattling song in April and May betrays its presence.

Passage migrant on the Deep Bay Marshes; April, May, October.

(**SPECKLED SEDGE-WARBLER** *Acrocephalus sorgophilus*, 5 ", probably indistinguishable from Von Schrenck's Reed-Warbler in the field; probably winters in S.E. China.)

(**SWINHOE'S REED-WARBLER (BLUNT-WINGED WARBLER)** *Acrocephalus concinens*, 5 ", a small Reed-Warbler with prominent white superciliary, which should distinguish it from Styan's Grasshopper Warbler; winters in S.E. China.)

280.　GREAT REED-WARBLER　　　　　　Plate 31.
Acrocephalus arundinaceus

大　葦　鶯

7½″.　Rich brown, with buff superciliary stripe, heavy bill.
Buffish underparts; rump shaded chestnut.　A bird of reedbeds;
in flight resembles thrush in shape, with tail fanned.　Song a
tuneless jangle, like Von Schrenck's, but harsher.
Passage migrant, scarce in spring, common in autumn; May,
September, October.

(THICK-BILLED WARBLER *Phragmaticola aedon*, 7½″,
similar to Great Reed-Warbler, but thicker, shorter bill, and
rounder wings and tail; no superciliary stripe; winters in S.
China.)

281.　YELLOW-BELLIED WILLOW-WARBLER　　Plate 32.
　　　　(BUFF-THROATED WARBLER)
Phylloscopus subaffinis

棕　腹　柳　鶯

4″.　Olive-brown, with conspicuous yellow superciliary, dark
green eyestripe; yellow on carpal joint, and one yellow wingbar.　Underparts rusty yellow, paler on throat.
Occasional visitor (normally entirely montane, above 4,000 ft.);
September.

(RADDE'S WARBLER *Phylloscopus schwarzi*, 4½″, could occur; resembles Dusky, but has some yellow on flanks, vent, and
carpal joint; much longer superciliary; brownish pectoral band
on some; inhabits pine forests, bushes, tall trees; call a harsh
'chick'.)

282.　DUSKY WARBLER *Phylloscopus fuscatus*　　Plate 32.
褐　柳　鶯

5″.　A skulking warbler of marshy areas and thick undergrowth.
Brown with a buff superciliary, underparts dull yellowish-brown,
darker on flanks and vent.　Usually recognised by its call, a
sharp 'tic, tic, tic'.
Winter visitor, mainly to the Deep Bay Marshes; September to
May.

283.　YELLOW-BROWED WARBLER　　　　　Plate 32.
　　　　(INORNATE WARBLER) *Phylloscopus inornatus*
黃　眉　柳　鶯

4″.　Olive-green, with yellowish superciliary, two yellow wingbars (sometimes occluded); underparts white.　Some have faint
coronal stripe.　Plump.　Call a plaintive 'wheet'.　Spends its

time in the upper branches of trees, very active, often in small parties. Often sings in March (loud but tuneless).

Winter visitor, found in almost all woods; September to May.

284. PALLAS'S WARBLER   Plate 32.
(LEMON-RUMPED WARBLER)
Phylloscopus proregulus
黃 腰 柳 鶯

3½". Bright olive-green, with bright yellow coronal, superciliary, and rump, and two wingbars. Call as Yellow-browed, but more clearly dissyllabic. Habits as Yellow-browed, but may immediately be distinguished by its much brighter colouration. Often hovers to feed.

Winter visitor; October to March.

(GREENISH WARBLER *Phylloscopus trochiloides*, (? = *plumbeitarsus*), 4½", may occur; very similar to Yellow-browed, but slightly larger; only one wingbar; darker legs and less pronounced superciliary than Arctic.)

285. ARCTIC WARBLER *Phylloscopus borealis*   Plate 32.
極 北 柳 鶯

4½". Olive-green, with yellowish superciliary and one wingbar, with sometimes traces of a second, but both may be completely occluded. Larger size, longer, thinner appearance is best distinction from Yellow-browed. Breast often greyish. Normally in ones and twos.

Passage migrant; April, May, September, October.

286. PALE-LEGGED WILLOW-WARBLER   Plate 32.
(PALE-LEGGED LEAF-WARBLER)
Phylloscopus tenellipes
灰 脚 柳 鶯

4¼". Olive-brown, with long whitish superciliary, dark streak through the eye, yellow patch on carpal joint. Underparts white, greenish on flanks, yellowish on vent. Double wingbar. Rusty rump and tail are the safest identification marks. Skulks in undergrowth. Most *Phylloscopus* warblers forage steadily through the trees, but Pale-legged stays longer in one place, then moves twenty or thirty yards to the next feeding area. Greyish head, pale grey breast. Call a metallic 'click'.

Passage migrant, sometimes wintering; April, September, October.
(IJIMA'S WILLOW-WARBLER *Phylloscopus ijimae* is very similar to Pale-legged in habits and call, but is greenish-olive

Plate 31

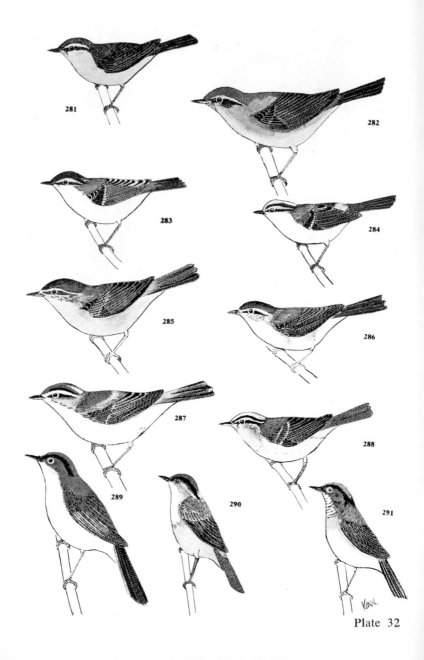

Plate 32

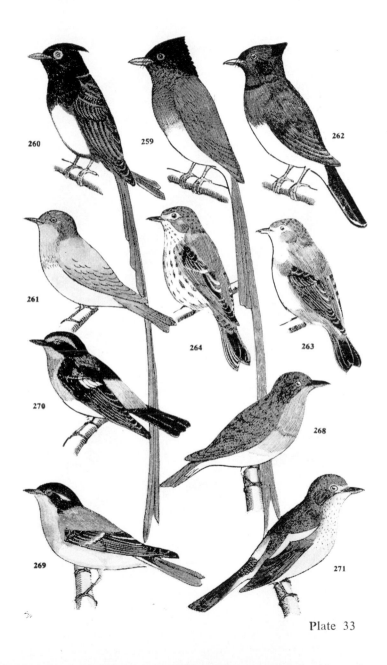

Plate 33

Plate 34

instead of brownish-olive; single wingbar; sometimes considered conspecific with *P. tenellipes;* this may occur here.)

287. CROWNED WILLOW-WARBLER Plate 32.
(EASTERN CROWNED WARBLER)
Phylloscopus coronatus

晃 柳 鶯

5″. Olive green, browner in spring; pale yellow superciliary, pale green coronal stripe, though not as well defined as Pallas's; wings with one clear bar, one indistinct bar; under wing-coverts and axillaries yellow; underparts white with a yellowish wash, particularly on vent. Large bill. Prefers deciduous woodland. Occasional visitor; October to March.

288. SULPHUR-BREASTED WARBLER Plate 32.
Phylloscopus ricketti

黃 胸 柳 鶯

4″. Bright green; coronal and superciliary yellow, separated by broad black bands; eyestripe black; underparts uniform bright yellow, which distinguish it immediately from all other *Phylloscopus* warblers. Double wingbar.

Six records (*P. cantator,* listed in the Annotated Checklist (1960, 1966), is a Himalayan form closely related to *P. ricketti*); November to March.

289. YELLOW-EYED FLYCATCHER-WARBLER Plate 32.
(GOLDEN-SPECTACLED WARBLER)
Seicercus burkii

金 眶 鷦 鶯

4½″. Upperparts bright olive-green, with two broad black coronal stripes; underparts bright yellow; conspicuous yellow eyering and greenish-yellow sides of head are distinctions from all other Flycatcher-Warblers. Titlike in behaviour.

One record; December 1960.

290. CHESTNUT-CROWNED WARBLER Plate 32.
Seicercus castaniceps

栗 頭 鷦 鶯

3½″. Upperparts green, with primaries darker; two yellow wingbars. Crown chestnut; two black coronal stripes; sides of head and throat battleship-grey; rest of underparts bright yellow. Very active.

One record; February to March, 1972.

291. FULVOUS-FACED FLYCATCHER-WARBLER Plate 32.
(RUFOUS-FACED WARBLER)
Seicercus albogularis

棕臉鶲鶯

3½ ". Forehead and sides of head light chestnut; two black coronal stripes; olive-green above, browner on the wings, with primrose-yellow rump. Underparts white, except for throat which is blackish mixed with white, and yellow breast and under tail-coverts.

Two records; February, November.

292. LONG-TAILED TAILOR-BIRD
(COMMON TAILORBIRD)   Plate 31.
Orthotomus sutorius

裁 縫 鳥

4½ ". Chestnut forehead and forecrown, pale buff superciliary, green upperparts, and very long tail (frequently cocked) are diagnostic. Found in undergrowth and thick bushes. Nests by riveting edges of a large leaf together, and building nests of grass, etc., inside the cup so formed; April to July. Calls varied but always monotonous.

Common resident.

293. DAVID'S HILL-WARBLER (BROWN PRINIA)
Prinia polychroa   Plate 31.

褐山鷦鶯

6". Dark brown above, almost blackish, streaked paler; long tail. Underparts buffish, olive wash on breast, fulvous on flanks and vent. Some barring on sides of breast in spring. Very dark plumage, and streaking on upperparts, distinguish from Yellow-bellied, which shares the same habitat. Grassy mountains above 2,000 ft. Nest as other *Prinias*.

Resident on Tai Mo Shan.

294. BROWN WREN-WARBLER   Plate 31.
(TAWNY-FLANKED PRINIA) *Prinia subflava*

褐頭鷦鶯

5½ ". Upperparts brown, underparts buffish; faint superciliary extending well behind eye; long tail. Found only on the Deep Bay Marshes. Length of superciliary is best distinction from Yellow-bellied Wren-Warbler. Nests low down in reeds or sea holly; domed nest; May to July.

Resident on the Deep Bay Marshes.

295. YELLOW-BELLIED WREN-WARBLER   Plate 31.
((YELLOW-BELLIED PRINIA)
Prinia flaviventris
灰頭鷦鶯

5½". Upperparts brown, with grey crown in summer; underparts pale buff, with yellow breast and belly on fully adult birds; long tail. Short, distinct pale line from bill to eye and pale eyering. In winter or immature plumage, very difficult to distinguish from the Brown Wren-Warbler. Fairly widespread, but prefers marshy ground. Call a plaintive mew, like a kitten. Nest similar to Brown Wren-Warbler.
Resident.

296. WHITE-BROWED HILL-WARBLER   Plate 31.
(HILL PRINIA) *Prinia atrogularis*
黑喉山鷦鶯

5½". Dark brown, with long white superciliary, and blackish eyestripe; chin very white, underparts buffish, fulvous on flanks and vent. Breast streaked with blackish especially on the sides. Grassy mountainsides.
One record; January 1961.

297. FANTAIL WARBLER (ZITTING CISTICOLA) Plate 31.
Cisticola juncidis
棕扇尾鶯

4". Rich chestnut, heavily streaked, especially on the crown. Short tail, with subterminal black band and buff tips. A marsh bird, seen most often in flight, when it makes a continuous ticking call; this is diagnostic. Nest similar to the *Prinias*; May, June.
Resident, mainly on the Deep Bay Marshes.

CHATS and THRUSHES: Turdidae

Longish, pointed bills; mainly woodland birds, generally with good songs; mainly migratory. Many species, especially genus Turdus, feed on the ground but, when disturbed, fly up to the treetops. Immatures generally have plumage similar to females.

298. JAPANESE ROBIN *Erithacus akahige*   Plate G.
日本歌鴝

5". Male has reddish-chestnut upperparts, brighter on head; orange throat divided from grey breast by black line; white underparts. Female is browner, the throat and breast less bright, and lacking the black line. Plump and upright; skulking. Generally in woodland undergrowth.
Two records; January to March.

299. RED-TAILED ROBIN   Plate G.
      (RUFOUS-TAILED ROBIN) *Erithacus sibilans*

紅 尾 歌 鴝

5″. Brown above, white below; reddish tail; necklace of crescent-shaped brown marks across breast. Upright; keeps to floor of woodlands.

Winter visitor; October to March.

300. BLUETHROAT *Erithacus svecicus*   Plate G.

藍 點 頦

5½″. Upperparts brown; tail dark brown with chestnut patch either side of base of tail, very conspicuous in flight. Whitish superciliary. In full plumage, male has blue patch, with central red spot, on throat; female has white throat with blackish necklace below it. Secretive; chestnut on tail is the usual recognition feature. Generally in marshy areas or farmland.

Scarce passage migrant and winter visitor; December to March.

301. SIBERIAN BLUE ROBIN *Erithacus cyane*   Plate G.

藍 歌 鴝

5½″. Rich blue upperparts, black line from bill to sides of breast, and white underparts, distinguish male. Female dull brown above, white below, with brown scales on breast. Forest undergrowth.

One record, April 1973.

302. (SIBERIAN) RUBYTHROAT *Erithacus calliope* Plate G.

紅 點 頦

5½″. Upperparts olive-brown; white superciliary and moustache-stripe; black in front of eye, and black stripe below moustache-stripe; chin and throat bright ruby-red, divided from whitish underparts by black line. In female, white stripes are not as distinct, and black markings replaced by brown; throat is white. A very skulking bird of thick undergrowth, usually located by plaintive whistle, but rarely seen.

Winter visitor; October to March.

303. RED-FLANKED BLUETAIL   Plate G.
      (ORANGE-FLANKED BUSH-ROBIN) *Tarsiger cyanurus*

紅脇藍尾鴝

5½″. Adult male is blue above, with brownish wings, orange flanks, white stripe across forehead and above eyes, white underparts. Female and immature brown, with pale orange flanks, white underparts, and bluish-grey tail; pale eyering. First-winter male sometimes distinguishable by faint white superciliary. Upright and flycatcher-like in appearance. Normally in woodland clearings; call 'tic-tic'.

Winter visitor, mainly immatures; October to March.

304. MAGPIE ROBIN *Copsychus saularis*　　　Plate G.
豬 屎 鵯

8″. Black, with white wingbar, abdomen and outer rectrices; female greyer. A bird of gardens and semi-cultivated areas; good song; chattering alarm-notes. Nests in holes, usually low down; April to July.

Common resident.

305. DAURIAN REDSTART *Phoenicurus auroreus*　Plate G.
灰頂紅尾鴝

5½″. Male has crown and nape pale grey; head, breast, back, wings, and central rectrices black. Conspicuous white patch on wing. Rump, outer rectrices, and underparts orange. Female is brown above, with small white wingpatch, dull orange rump and outer rectrices; underparts whitish, orange-brown on flanks. Characteristically "shivers" its tail.

Winter visitor in open country, favouring hedges and disused paddy; October to March.

306. PLUMBEOUS WATER-REDSTART　　　　　　Plate G.
(PLUMBEOUS REDSTART) *Rhyacornis fuliginosus*
紅 尾 水 鴝

5″. Adult male bluish-slate above, wings blackish-brown; tail and vent bright chestnut-red; underparts grey. Female and first-winter male bluish-grey, scalloped olive; underparts similar but greyer; white rump. Normally seen on a rock in the middle of a swift-flowing mountain-stream; flicks tail repeatedly; sallies forth like a flycatcher.

Scarce winter visitor, adult males rare; December to March.

307. WHITE-CAPPED REDSTART (RIVER CHAT)
　　　　Thamnolaea leucocephala　　　　　　　　Plate G.
白 頂 溪 鴝

7″. Gleaming white crown; rest of head, breast, and wings black; back, rump, tail, and underparts deep rich orange; dark subterminal bar on tail. Frequents swift mountain streams.

One record, February to April 1974.

308. STONECHAT *Saxicola torquata* **Plate 34.**

黑 喉 石 鵖

5″. Plump and upright, a bird of open heaths, fields, and marshes; summer male has black head and throat, white half-collar and wingbar, whitish rump; rest of upperparts brown, underparts chestnut, shading to buff on vent. In other plumages, little or no black on head, upperparts brown, slight eyestripe, underparts buffish. Perches on tops of bushes, constantly jerking its tail.

Common winter visitor and passage migrant; September to April.

309. GREY BUSHCHAT *Saxicola ferrea* **Plate 34.**

灰 林 鵖

5″. Male grey, with blackish wings; white superciliary and black cheeks; underparts pale grey to white. Female brown, chestnut on rump and tail, with darker cheeks; abdomen paler. Usually perched on low bushes near the edge of woods. Constantly flicks wings and jerks tail like Stonechat.

Winter visitor; November to March.

310. BLUE ROCKTHRUSH *Monticola solitarius* **Plate 35.**

藍 磯 鶇

8″. Adult male is deep blue-grey, with lower breast and underparts chestnut-red on some specimens. Two races are involved, one with red belly, the other without, and there are numerous intermediates. Females and young birds have plumage bluish brown, closely barred or scalloped above and below. Characteristically perches on a roof or a prominent rock, and flicks its tail constantly.

Both races are winter visitors; October to March.

311. CHESTNUT-BREASTED ROCKTHRUSH **Plate 35.**
(CHESTNUT-BELLIED ROCKTHRUSH)
Monticola rufiventris

栗 胸 磯 鶇

8½″. Male similar to red-bellied form of Blue Rockthrush, but chestnut of belly extends to cover whole breast; upperparts brighter blue; breast of female is buffish. Female has almost white throat. Habits as Blue Rockthrush.

Eight or more records; December to April.

312. VIOLET WHISTLING THRUSH (BLUE WHISTLING THRUSH)
Plate G.

Myiophonus caeruleus

紫 嘯 鶇

12″. Blackish violet with pale tips to feathers (looks spotted with white); colouration can apparently change from black to blue and pale violet according to light; black bill. Fans tail frequently. Preference for mountain streams Nests on ledges or trees near streams; April to June. High-pitched whistling notes are frequently heard.
Resident.

313. PALE THRUSH *Turdus pallidus*
Plate 35.

白 腹 鶇

9″. Male has grey head and breast, brown upperparts, darker on wings and tail; white chin, brown breast and flanks, whitish abdomen. Female is paler, with white chin, brown band across breast. Both sexes most easily distinguishable in flight by whitish tips of outer rectrices. Only immatures have any noticeable streaking (on underparts only).
Scarce winter visitor; December to March.

314. EYEBROWED THRUSH *Turdus obscurus*
Plate 35.

白 眉 鶇

7½″. White eyebrow, prominent on male, less so on female, is diagnostic. Head grey, upperparts brown. Male has white chin, orange breast and flanks, white abdomen, unspotted; female has white throat, spotted, and some streaking on breast; flanks duller than male.
Scarce winter visitor; January to April.

315. BROWN THRUSH (BROWN-HEADED THRUSH)
Turdus chysolaus
Plate 35.

赤 腹 鶇

8″. Olive-brown above; cheek dark on male, paler on female; throat dusky-brown on male, whitish and streaked on female. Breast and flanks deep orange-chestnut. Abdomen white. Lack of superciliary distinguishes it from Eyebrowed Thrush.
Rare winter visitor; December to February.

316. GREY-BACKED THRUSH *Turdus hortulorum* Plate 35.

灰 背 鶇

7½″. Male has grey upperparts and breast, orange flanks, no streaking. Female is browner, with streaking on breast and flanks (see Grey Thrush). Centre of breast and abdomen whitish.
Common winter visitor; October to April.

317. DUSKY THRUSH *Turdus naumanni eunomus* **Plate 35.**

斑 鶇

9″. Upperparts dark brown, heavily spotted and with much chestnut; rump and base of tail chestnut. Prominent superciliary is white. Throat white, spotted brown; blackish band across breast, scalloped white. Rest of underparts white, heavily spotted black on flanks. Females and young birds are similar, but show less chestnut. Seen in open fields, rarely in woods. A more northerly subspecies, *T. n. naumanni*, which has red instead of black across the breast, and a reddish chestnut tail, and is generally paler above and slightly smaller, has occurred twice.

Irregular winter visitor; November to March.

318. (COMMON) BLACKBIRD *Turdus merula* **Plate 35.**

烏 鶇

10″. Male black, with yellow bill; female dark brown, with yellowish-brown bill. In small flocks, frequently in treetops; noisy but shy; behaviour and calls unlike English Blackbird, although this is the same species.

Winter visitor; October to March.

319. GREY THRUSH (JAPANESE THRUSH) **Plate 35.**
Turdus cardis

烏 灰 鶇

7½″. Male dark grey, almost black, above and on breast, clearly demarcated from white abdomen, which is spotted with black on lower breast and flanks. Yellow bill. Female has brown upperparts; breast spotted black; varying amounts of orange on flanks and breast; not usually safely distinguishable in the field from female Grey-backed Thrush.

Winter visitor; October to April.

320. SIBERIAN THRUSH *Zoothera sibirica* **Plate 35.**

白 眉 地 鶇

9″. Male black, slightly paler on abdomen; prominent white eyestripe. White bar across underside of wing (both sexes) only visible in flight; young males have white abdomen. Female olive-green, underparts buff with narrow speckled band of brown across upper breast; abdomen white.

Five records; October to April.

Plate 35

Plate 36

321. ORANGE-HEADED GROUND-THRUSH Plate 35.
(ORANGE-HEADED THRUSH) *Zoothera citrina*

橙 頭 地 鶇

7½″. Male has head, neck, chest, and flanks orange; lores and cheeks whitish; upperparts blue-grey; abdomen and vent white. Female is browner above, paler below.
About six records; October to April.

322. WHITE'S THRUSH (SCALY THRUSH) Plate 35.
Zoothera dauma

虎 斑 山 鶇

10½″. Golden-brown above, heavily speckled darker; underparts white, barred black on throat, breast, and flanks. Underside of wing shows broad black and white wingbar in flight. Long legs characteristic. Flight rapid, usually close to ground. Generally in clearings, paths, or at edges of woods.
Scarce winter visitor; December to March.

DIPPERS: Cinclidae

323. BROWN DIPPER *Cinclus pallasii* Plate 30.

褐 河 烏

8″. Chocolate-brown, darker below. Whitish eyering, not very conspicuous. Stubby tail. A bird of swift mountain streams, where it perches on a rock, bobbing up and down; sometimes walks off into the water, and can walk under water; flight rapid, with wings moving very fast.
Two records; April, August.

WRENS: Troglodytidae

324. (NORTHERN) WREN *Troglodytes troglodytes* Plate 30.

鷦 鷯

3¾″. Tiny, plump; brown, with slight eyestripe, and short tail, usually cocked almost vertical. Forages on forest floor. Call a sharp 'tic-tic-tic'. Easily confused with Short-tailed Bush-Warbler, but distinguished by longer tail, heavy mottling on upperparts and breast, and lack of long white superciliary which is very conspicuous on the Short-tailed Bush-Warbler.
No recent records; status obscure due to confusion with the Short-tailed Bush-Warbler.

TITS: Aegithalidae and Paridae

Active plump little birds of woodlands. Generally move through woods in parties, calling constantly to keep in contact.

325. GREAT TIT *Parus major*   Plate 34.
白臉山雀

5½". Upperparts grey, underparts dull white. Black crown
and bib, joined by line running from from nape to top of bib,
and black line down centre of abdomen. White cheeks and spot
on nape. Young birds are yellower below, have yellowish-
brown in place of black on head and throat. Great variety of
calls. Gregarious in winter. Nests in holes; February to May.
Common resident.

326. YELLOW-BELLIED TIT *Parus venustulus*   Plate 34.
黃腹山雀

4½". Male has head and throat black, white cheek, white
patch on nape; upperparts grey, with black primaries; two white
wingbars, composed of spots; underparts bright yellow. Females
and young have the same general pattern, but the black is replaced by olive, and the white by pale yellow; underparts also
pale yellow. One wing-bar in flight. Call a constant high-
pitched 'si-si-si-si-si', much higher than any Great Tit call.
Gregarious. Normally a montane species.
Many, winters 1969-70 and 1971-2 only; November to April.

327. RED-HEADED TIT (BLACK-THROATED TIT)
       Aegithalos concinnus   Plate 34.
紅頭山雀

4". Reddish-chestnut cap, rest of upperparts blue-grey. Chin
and underparts white, with black cheek-patch, and large black
bib; band of chestnut across the breast, and fulvous on flanks
and vent; long tail. Gregarious; normally in mountainous areas.
One record; April 1960.

PIPITS and WAGTAILS: Motacillidae

Ground-haunting birds; pipits are brown and streaked, prefer
grassy areas. Wagtails have long tails, are pied or with much
yellow in plumage, usually found near water. All pipits have
white outer rectrices, except Petchora.

328. RICHARD'S PIPIT *Anthus novaeseelandiae*   Plate 27.
田 鷚

6½-7". A large pipit, upright and long-legged. Sandy upperparts, streaked brownish; breast lightly streaked; underparts
otherwise pale buff. Legs pink. One race, a summer visitor
in Hong Kong, is considerably darker. Soars like a lark. Nests
on ground; April to June.
Summer and winter visitor.

329. INDIAN TREE-PIPIT (OLIVE TREE-PIPIT) Plate 27.
Anthus hodgsoni

樹 鷚

5½". Dark brown, streaked above; underparts buffish with breast and flanks heavily streaked black. Legs pink. Feeds on ground below trees in open woodland, generally pines; flies up into branches when disturbed. Rump not streaked. Tail constantly bobbed up and down. Call a thin 'tsip, tsip, tsip'. Winter visitor; October to April.

330. RED-THROATED PIPIT *Anthus cervinus* Plate 27.

紅 喉 鷚

5¾". In spring, varying amounts of red on neck and throat are diagnostic; red may be more or less spotted with brown. In winter, this is a dark pipit found in the same areas as Richard's, but comparatively short-legged, and heavily streaked on breast and flanks. Rump boldly streaked. Upperparts very mottled in some plumages, especially in spring. Thin high-pitched call. **ROSY PIPIT** *Anthus roseatus*, which may occur, is greyer on upperparts; dark brown ear-coverts are conspicuous in spring plumage.
Passage migrant and winter visitor, generally in marshy areas or paddy; October to April.

331. PETCHORA PIPIT *Anthus gustavi* Plate 27.

北 鷚

6". Easily confused with Indian Tree-Pipit, but it prefers open grassland. Associates with Red-throated Pipit, from which it is distinguished in all plumages by two pale streaks down back from nape to rump. Outer tail-feathers, buffish, not white. Rump streaked. Heavily streaked breast.
One record; February 1971.

332. WATER PIPIT *Anthus spinoletta* Plate 27.

水 鷚

6½". Closest to Red-throated Pipit, but upperparts greyer, less brown, less streaked. Prominent buff superciliary. This is the only pipit with dark legs. Spotted rather than streaked on underparts.
Scarce passage migrant or winter visitor, in open marshy areas; November to February.

333. UPLAND PIPIT *Anthus sylvanus* Plate 27.

山 鷚

7". Similar to Richard's Pipit, but much darker, and underparts spotted rather than streaked. Found only on bare mountains. Low darting flight when flushed is helpful characteristic; Richard's usually flies much higher. Nests on ground; April to July.

Resident on all the higher mountainsides, above 1,500 feet.

334. FOREST WAGTAIL *Dendronanthus indicus* **Plate 27.**
林 鶺 鴒

5½″. Grey-brown upperparts, with two bars of white on blackish wing. Whitish superciliary. Underparts white, with double black band across breast. Wags tail from side to side as it walks along ground or branch. Generally in woodlands. Passage migrant; April, September, October.

335. WHITE WAGTAIL *Motacilla alba* **Plate 27.**
白 鶺 鴒

7″. Upperparts black and grey; white cheeks, some birds with black eyestripe; prominent black bib; underparts white. In winter, black is replaced by grey. Call 'ti-zik'.

Winter visitor; perhaps breeds occasionally; September to May.

336. GREY WAGTAIL *Motacilla cinerea* **Plate 27.**
灰 鶺 鴒

7½″. Grey upperparts, yellow underparts, brightest on vent; very long black tail with white outer rectrices. Male has black throat in summer. Usually seen on streams, where it flits from rock to rock, wagging its tail persistently. Call 'tseet-tseet'.

Winter visitor; August to May.

337. YELLOW WAGTAIL *Motacilla flava* **Plate 27.**
黃 鶺 鴒

7″. Olive-green above, buffish below in winter. Long tail marks it as a wagtail, and there is usually some yellow on underparts. In summer plumage, all underparts and sides of head are bright yellow, with dark eyestripe and crown. Plumage very variable. Call 'tsoo-eep'. Marshy and low-lying areas. Passage migrant and winter visitor; September to May.

338. YELLOW-HEADED WAGTAIL **Plate 38.**
(YELLOW-HOODED WAGTAIL) *Motacilla citreola*
黃 頭 鶺 鴒

6½″. Summer male has head, neck and underparts unmarked canary-yellow; black hind-collar, blue-grey upperparts. Distinguished from Yellow Wagtail in all plumages by two white wingbars.

One record; September.

SUNBIRDS: Nectariniidae

339. FORK-TAILED SUNBIRD *Aethopyga christinae* **Plate 36.**

义尾太陽鳥

3½-4″. Male has crown and nape bright metallic green, rest of upperparts dark olive-green, with light yellow rump; chin to upper breast bright crimson; rest of underparts pale yellowish. Female is green above, yellowish-green on breast, yellowish abdomen. Male has central rectrices extended in pins ½″ beyond rest of tail. Bill long and decurved. Although colouration resembles flowerpeckers, slim shape should distinguish it at once. Call of male a metallic 'chiff-chiff-chiff'. Nest a ball of grass, usually about ten feet up in a tree; May to June. Resident.

WHITE-EYES: Zosteropidae

340. (JAPANESE) WHITE-EYE *Zosterops japonica* **Plate 36.**

相 思 雀

3½-4″. Bright green above, greenish-yellow below, with white abdomen; sometimes with some orange on throat and flanks. White eyering conspicuous. Gregarious in winter. Flocks call to each other constantly, a tinkling note. Flocks often associate with Great Tits and *Phylloscopus* warblers. Nests in small trees and bamboo; cup built of grass and moss; March to August. Resident and winter visitor.

(**CHESTNUT-FLANKED WHITE-EYE** *Zosterops erythropleura*, 4″, similar to White-Eye, but distinguished by bright chestnut flanks; throat yellow; rest of underparts white; one record in November 1970 could be of wild birds.)

FLOWERPECKERS: Dicaeidae

Tiny plump birds with short tails, often brightly coloured; their presence usually recognised by the clicking call uttered in flight. Generally keep to tall trees.

341. SCARLET-BACKED FLOWERPECKER **Plate 36.**
   Dicaeum cruentatum

朱背啄花雀

3″. Crown and back down to rump, bright scarlet on male; wings, sides of head, and breast black; underparts pale olive. Female is olive-green above, paler below, with scarlet upper tail-coverts. Domed nest placed near the end of a high branch of a tree; June to August. Resident.

342. FIRE-BREASTED FLOWERPECKER   Plate 36.
(BUFF-BELLIED FLOWERPECKER)
Dicaeum ignipectus

紅胸啄花雀

3″. Male dark blue-green above, black head and breast; patch of bright crimson in centre of breast; rest of underparts buff, with a black central stripe. Female is olive-green above, buff below, with no red markings.

Winter visitor; October to March.

FINCHES: Fringillidae

Small seed-eating birds characterised by stout triangular bills.

343. BLACK-TAILED HAWFINCH   Plate H.
(YELLOW-BILLED GROSBEAK)
Coccothraustes migratorius

黑尾蠟咀雀

7½″. Heavy, bright yellow bill, black head and wings of male, with prominent white wingbar; grey-brown upperparts with black tail, pale grey underparts. Female is duller, with no black on head. Generally in small flocks in open country with scattered woods.

Winter visitor; November to March.

344. CHINESE GREENFINCH   Plate H.
(GREY-CAPPED GREENFINCH) *Carduelis sinica*

金 翅 雀

5″. Greenish above and below, with greyish head, brown wings, yellow rump, under tail-coverts, and prominent wingbar. Female and young duller. Slightly forked tail. Gregarious out of the breeding season. Constant twittering call. Nest a cup built of grass and fibres in bushes or trees; March to June.
Resident.

(BLACK-HEADED GREENFINCH *Carduelis ambigua*, 5″, as Chinese Greenfinch but whole head black on male, dark brown on female; yellow wingbars and tail-patch conspicuous. One record, presumably escapes.)

(BRAMBLING *Fringilla montifringilla*, 6″, black head, neck, wings, and back; white rump and belly; reddish-brown breast and flanks; female is duller, with brownish head and back; often feeds on the ground; at least two records, probably escapes.)

345. (EURASIAN) SISKIN *Carduelis spinus*   **Plate H.**

黃 雀

4¾″. A bright yellow-green finch, streaked black, with a black crown and chin on the male, yellow breast, yellow rump, and short stubby bill; female duller; forked tail. A common cagebird, hence our records, well south of normal winter range, were suspect until several flocks occurred in winter 1972-73.

346. COMMON ROSEFINCH   **Plate H.**
      Carpodacus erythrinus

朱 雀

5¾″. Male has brilliant rose-carmine head, breast, and rump, dark brown wings and tail, and pinkish underparts; female brown, streaked, nondescript; slightly forked tail. Female is only brown, streaked finch in Hong Kong. Usually in small flocks in open country.

Winter visitor; November to March.

BUNTINGS: Emberizidae

Similar to finches; generally on or near the ground; white outer tail-feathers on all species except Crested distinguish from all other groups except larks and pipits, both of which have slender bills. Most species tend to skulk.

347. MASKED BUNTING (BLACK-FACED BUNTING)
      Emberiza spodocephala   **Plate 37.**

灰 頭 鵐

5½-6″. Adult male has grey head with darker eyepatch, streaked brown upperparts, and lemon-yellow underparts, much streaked. Females, nondescript, best recognised by total absence of any marked characteristics. This is usually the common bunting of Hong Kong in winter, but it tends to skulk; not normally in thick woodland.

Winter visitor; October to April.

348. TRISTRAM'S BUNTING *Emberiza tristrami*   **Plate 37.**

白 鵰 鵐

5½″. Black and white 'bull's-eye' head of male, and bright chestnut upperparts, especially rump, are diagnostic. Underparts are buff, white on abdomen. Females have brown instead of black on head, buff instead of white. A bird of forest undergrowth, normally seen in small parties. Call a soft 'chip'.

Winter visitor; November to March.

349. CHESTNUT BUNTING *Emberiza rutila*   Plate 37.
栗　鵐

5″. Male has head, upperparts, and breast bright chestnut, yellow underparts. Female is duller, with some streaks on underparts. Generally in small parties; undergrowth of swampy forest preferred, but will also frequent paddy and open marshland.

Scarce passage migrant; April, December.

350. YELLOW-BREASTED BUNTING   Plate 37.
    Emberiza aureola

黄　胸　鵐

5½″. White patch on wings in both sexes diagnostic. Upperparts chestnut, streaked. Yellow underparts. Male has blackish head, and chestnut band across breast; female has usual bunting head-pattern. Normally in flocks on paddy or marshes.

Passage migrant; April, October, November.

351. YELLOW-BROWED BUNTING   Plate 37.
    Emberiza chrysophrys

黄　鶥　鵐

6″. Narrow white coronal stripe, separated by black stripes from long bright yellow superciliary. Upperparts brown, streaked; chin and malar stripe black; underparts whitish, with dark streaks on breast and flanks. Female similar but duller. A bird of pine forests.

One record; December 1931.

352. SIEBOLD'S BUNTING   Plate 37.
  (JAPANESE YELLOW BUNTING)
    Emberiza sulphurata

硫　黄　鵐

5″. Black lores, whitish eyering, slight yellow eyebrow. Upperparts olive-green, unstreaked on head and neck, but darker and heavily streaked on wings. Chin dark green, underparts lemon yellow, greener on breast and flanks. Habitat and habits as Masked Bunting.

One shot by Swinhoe in 1860.

353. GREY-HEADED BUNTING   Plate 37.
  (CHESTNUT-EARED BUNTING)
    Emberiza fucata

赤　胸　鵐

5½-6″. Head grey, streaked black; chestnut cheek-patches; black moustache-stripe joined to black band across breast (more or less composed of spots); a narrow chestnut band across buffish

Plate 37

Plate 38

PARTS OF A BIRD

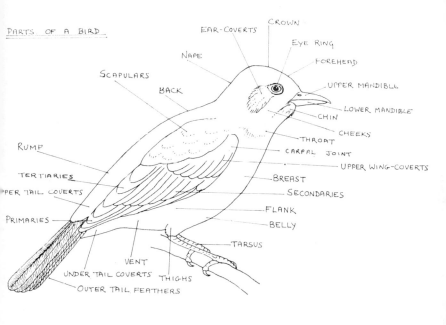

- CROWN
- EAR-COVERTS
- EYE RING
- NAPE
- FOREHEAD
- SCAPULARS
- UPPER MANDIBLE
- BACK
- LOWER MANDIBLE
- CHIN
- CHEEKS
- THROAT
- CARPAL JOINT
- RUMP
- UPPER WING-COVERTS
- TERTIARIES
- BREAST
- UPPER TAIL COVERTS
- SECONDARIES
- PRIMARIES
- FLANK
- BELLY
- TARSUS
- VENT
- UNDER TAIL COVERTS
- THIGHS
- OUTER TAIL FEATHERS

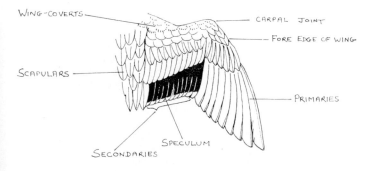

- WING-COVERTS
- CARPAL JOINT
- FORE EDGE OF WING
- SCAPULARS
- PRIMARIES
- SPECULUM
- SECONDARIES

UPPER WING OF DUCK

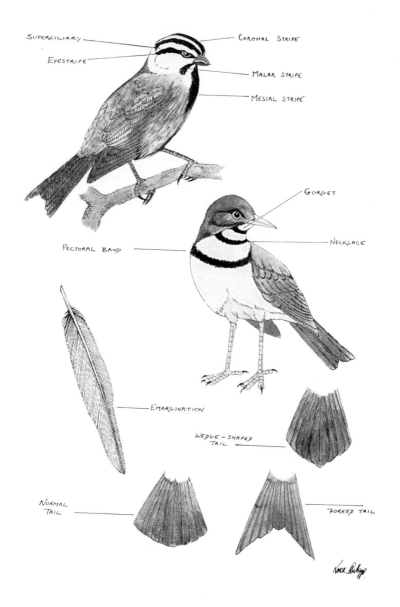

SUPERCILIARY

EYESTRIPE

CORONAL STRIPE

MALAR STRIPE

MESIAL STRIPE

GORGET

NECKLACE

PECTORAL BAND

EMARGINATION

WEDGE-SHAPED TAIL

NORMAL TAIL

FORKED TAIL

belly. Upperparts chestnut-brown, pale chestnut rump conspicuous in flight. Female duller and browner. Normally in marshy grassland.

354. LITTLE BUNTING   Plate 37.
Emberiza pusilla

小　鵐

5¼". Crown and cheeks chestnut, boldly outlined in black; upperparts brown and streaked; underparts white, streaked black on sides of throat, breast, and flanks. Black on head not always distinct, but this species should always be recognisable by chestnut cheeks, though these are duller in winter; only other bunting with these is Grey-headed, which has characteristic breast markings. Usually in open, marshy country.

Winter visitor; November to April.

(RUSTIC BUNTING *Emberiza rustica*, 5½", has black head on male with white post-ocular stripe; head brown on female. Chestnut band across breast with otherwise white underparts is distinctive of both sexes. Two records 1975/6, probably both escapes.)

355. REED BUNTING *Emberiza schoeniclus*

藍　鵐

6". Male has black head and throat, white streak from bill to white collar. Remaining upperparts brown streaked blackish, underparts white, with some streaking on flanks. Female brown, with conspicuous black and white moustache streaks. Marshy areas.

One record, March 1975.

356. CRESTED BUNTING *Melophus lathami*   Plate 37.

鳳　頭　鵐

6". Male is black, with prominent black crest, and deep chestnut wings and tail. Female is duller, but also has slight crest, and is noticeably chestnut on wings.. A mountain bird, descending to valleys in winter. Perches on telegraph wires. Nest placed on ground, in tussock of grass; April to June.

Resident.

SPARROWS: Ploceidae

Small birds with heavy triangular bills; often in flocks. Flight of Munias direct and rapid, with very fast wingbeats.

357. (EURASIAN) TREE SPARROW — Plate H.
Passer montanus

麻 雀

5½″. Crown chestnut, upperparts brown, streaked darker; cheeks white, with a large black spot; chin black; underparts dirty white. Sexes alike. The common sparrow of town and country. Nest an untidy ball of grass, normally in a hole; March to August.
Abundant resident.

358. RUDDY SPARROW (RUSSET SPARROW) — Plate H.
Passer rutilans

山 麻 雀

5″. Similar to Tree Sparrow, but brighter chestnut above, and no black spot on cheek; blackish lores; female is duller, and has no black on chin. Double wingbar. Gregarious; a bird of mountains and open country.
One record; December 1960.
(BAYA WEAVER *Ploceus philippinus*, 6″, a brown streaked finchlike bird with heavy bill, and bright yellow crown and black face-patch on male; gregarious. Escapes sometimes occur.)

359. RED AVADAVAT *Amandava amandava* — Plate H.
紅梅花雀

3½-4″. A tiny crimson bird spotted with white; females and young are brown, with some crimson on wings and rump. Usually in small flocks.
Winter visitor, mainly to the Deep Bay Marshes; September to March. (Although this species is not known to breed in China, and is a common cage-bird, the regularity of its occurrence, always in areas well away from the city, strongly indicates that these are genuinely wild birds.)

360. JAVA SPARROW *Padda oryzivora* — Plate H.
禾 谷

5″. Black head with white cheeks, and large pink bill; upperparts and breast pale grey, darker on wings; abdomen white; flanks pale pinkish. Gregarious.
Status unknown; a common cage-bird, and many records are undoubtedly of escapes.

361. CHESTNUT MUNIA *Lonchura malacca* — Plate H.
栗腹文雀

4-4½″. Deep chestnut, with a black head. Pale blue bill. A white-bellied form occurs occasionally, probably escapes. Nest, a ball of grass low down in a bush; April to June.
Scarce summer visitor; April to October.

362. SPOTTED MUNIA (SCALY-BREASTED MUNIA)
Lonchura punctulata   **Plate H.**

斑 文 雀

4-4½ ". Upperparts brown, darker on wings, slightly barred on
rump; cheeks, chin, and throat deep brown; breast and flanks
scalloped with brown spots; rest of underparts white. Gregarious;
nest as Chestnut Munia, but often in trees; April to June.

Resident and winter visitor.

363. WHITE-BACKED MUNIA (WHITE-RUMPED MUNIA)
Lonchura striata   **Plate H.**

白 腰 文 雀

4-4½ ". Similar to Spotted Munia, but distinguished by darker
back, blackish chin, brighter brown spots on breast, white rump,
and black centre to pointed tail. Nest as Spotted Munia; April
to September.

Resident, perhaps commoner in winter.

(WHITE-HEADED MUNIA *Lonchura maja*, has white head
and neck, cinnamon to brown upperparts, and paler belly; the
few records are probably of escapes, as this is not a Chinese
species.)

Addenda

6a. STREAKED SHEARWATER *Calonectris leucomelas*
19″. Dark brown, with most of underside of wings white (brown trailing edge). Front half of crown appears white in field; darker streaks only visible at close range.
One record, a bird captured at Aberdeen in January 1977.

142a. PECTORAL SANDPIPER *Calidris melanotos* **Plate 15**
See p. 35. First reecorded in May 1976.

162a. LONG-TAILED SKUA (LONG-TAILED JAEGER)
Stercorarius longicaudus
長 尾 海 鷗
20″, including tail of almost half this length. Dark brown cap and upperparts (with some white at base of primaries), white collar and underparts, sometimes with dark breast-band. Yellow cheeks and side of neck. Very long slender extended centre tail-feathers are diagnostic of adult, though these are often broken off. Bill strong (gull-like) and black. Immatures are brown above and below. Tern-like flight. Maritime.
One record, May 1976.

(**HAWFINCH** *Coccothraustes coccothraustes*, 7″, distinguished by heavy greyish bill, black wings with conspicuous white shoulder-patch, more or less rufous upperparts and belly, whitish lower abdomen and tip to tail. One record, May 1976, probably an escape.)

Appendix I

Wing-formulae of warblers

For warblers in the hand, wing-formula is an important aid to identification. The following list gives the primaries in descending order of size, and details of emargination (notches on the outer web of the primaries). Note that the first primary is often very small. Many of these species are doubtfully separable in the field. Primaries are numbered from the outside inwards towards the secondaries.

(N.B.   e. = emarginated)

Phylloscopus	*proregulus*	4=5 3) 6) 7	e.6
	inornatus	4=3=5) 6) 7) 2	e.6
	coronatus	4=3) 5) 6) 2) 7	e.6 slight
	ricketti	3=4=5) 6) 7) 2	e.6
	borealis	3) 4) 5) 2) 6	no e.
	plumbeitarsus	4) 5) 3) 6) 7) 2	e.6 (Asian form of *trochiloides*)
	tenellipes	4) 3) 5) 6) 2) 7	e.6 slight
	ijimae	as *tenellipes*	
	fuscatus	4=5) 3=6) 7) 8) 2	e.6
	schwarzi	4=5) 3) 6 – 8) 2	e.6
	subaffinis	4=5) 3) 6 – 9) 2	
Locustella	*lanceolata*	3) 4=or) 2) 5	e.3
	certhiola	3) 4) 2=5) 6	e.3 sometimes 4
	ochotensis	3) 2=4) 5	e.3
	pleskei	4=3) 5) 2) 6	e.3
	fasciolata	3) 2) 4) 5	e.3
Acrocephalus	*bistrigiceps*	3=4) 5) 6) 2	e.3-5
	sorgophilus	4=3) 5) 2) 6	e.3-5
	concinens	4=5) 3) 6 – 8) 2	e.3-5 sometimes 6
	arundinaceus	3) 4) 2) 5	e.3 or 3-4
Phragmaticola	*aedon*	4) 3) 5 – 7) 2	e.3-5

Appendix II

Glossary

axillaries... a patch of feathers underneath where the wing joins the body (visible in flight)

carpal joint... the 'bend' of the wing

coronal stripe... stripe extending from the bill back lengthways along the crown of the head

crepuscular... active after dark

eclipse... a dull plumage, similar to that of females, adopted by male duck after the breeding season

emargination... cut away in a slanting direction; used particularly to describe the outer web of a primary narrowing suddenly towards the tip

eyestripe... a stripe from the bill through the eye

facial skin... a patch of bare skin between bill and eye

flanks... sides of the body, partly visible just below the wing when the bird is at rest

frontal shield... a bare patch of hardened skin, often brightly coloured, covering the base of the upper mandible and part of the forehead

gorget... like a necklace, but across the upper throat, quite near the bill

gular pouch... pouch of skin below the lower mandible (of a pelican)

irruptions... incursions of unusual numbers of a species, occurring irregularly

lores... patch of feathers between bill and eye

malar streak... a streak extending diagonally back and downwards from the base of the bill

mandible... either upper or lower section of the bill

mantle... back, wing-coverts and scapulars

melanistic... with black or grey replacing the normal pigment

mesial streak... a streak extending vertically down the throat from the base of the lower mandible

moustache stripe... same as malar streak

nape... the back of the head, where it joins the neck

necklace... a band across the lower throat

occluded... **hidden**

pectoral band... a band across the breast

plume... a narrow elongated feather, for display purposes; generally part of a breeding plumage (cf. egrets)

post-orbital... behind the eye

primaries... main flight-feathers on the wing

rectrices... main feathers of the tail

rump... lower end of the back, just above the tail

scalloped... with small crescent-shaped markings

scapulars... feathers overlapping the join between wing and body (above)

secondaries... the large feathers at the back (trailing edge) of the inner half of the wing

speculum... a coloured patch on the secondaries

superciliary... a stripe above the eye

tail-coverts... small feathers covering the base of the rectrices

tarsus... the name usually given to the lower part of a bird's leg, from the knee-joint to the ankle-joint

tertiaries... a name sometimes given to elongated inner secondaries

vent... when describing plumage, this refers to the under tail-coverts

vermiculated... closely marked with small curved markings

wattle... a piece of bare skin, often loose, and often brightly-coloured, on the head of a bird (cf. mynahs)

wedge-shaped... the tail is described as wedge-shaped when its shape, when spread, is roughly triangular with the central rectrices as the apex; this contrasts with a forked tail, when the central rectrices are shorter than the outer ones, or the normal tail shape, in which the tips of the rectrices form a curve.

wing-coverts... small feathers covering the bases of the primaries and secondaries

wing-formula... a method of describing the shape of a wing by listing the primaries in descending order of length

wing-lining... **under wing-coverts.**

Appendix III

Bibliography

The following are the chief works consulted in the preparation of this book. Those which are most useful here, and which should be obtained by any serious birdwatcher working in this area, are marked with an asterisk.

*Dement'ev and Gladkov (1965-70), Birds of the Soviet Union, English translation by the Israel Programme for Scientific Translations. 6 vols.

Herklots, G.A.C. (1967). Hong Kong Birds.

*King, Ben F., Woodcock, M., and Dickinson, E.C. (1975). Field Guide to the Birds of South-East Asia.

*Kobayashi, K. (1973). Birds of Japan in Natural Colours. Text in Japanese.

*La Touche, J.D.D. (1927-34). A Handbook of the Birds of Eastern China. 2 vols.

Macdonald and Macfarlane (1966). An Annotated Checklist of the Birds of Hong Kong, 2nd Edition.

*Peterson, R.T. et al. (1967). Field Guide to the Birds of Britain and Europe.

Salim Ali and S. Dillon Ripley (1970-74). Handbook of the Birds of India and Pakistan. 10 vols.

*Smythies, B.E. (1953). Birds of Burma.

*Smythies, B.E. (1960). Birds of Borneo.

Vaurie, C. (1959, 1965). Birds of the Palaearctic Fauna. 2 vols.

*Webster, M.A. (1975). An Annotated Checklist of the Birds of Hong Kong. 3rd Edition.

In addition the Annual Reports of the Hong Kong Bird Watching Society, from the first issue in 1958, have been used extensively

INDEX

(Plate numbers are in **bold type**)

目 錄